Like It Was Yesterday

THE STORY OF A GAME THAT WAS NEVER PLAYED... IN A TOWN THAT NEVER FORGOT.

———

Dennis R. Bender

ISBN-13: 9781548506445
ISBN-10: 1548506443
Library of Congress Control Number: 2017910466
CreateSpace Independent Publishing Platform
North Charleston, South Carolina

Like it Was Yesterday is dedicated to my Lord and Savior without whom I could not draw my next breath, much less write a book.
Dennis R Bender

Prologue

———

In the spring of 2007, I was reminiscing along with my lifelong friend Mike Petrolle. He mentioned he had always wanted to write a book about the 1954 Mont Pleasant High School vs. Nott Terrace High School football game that was supposed to take place in Schenectady, New York, and why it never was played. He said he had made a few starts, mostly using that non-event as the basis for a fictionalized story in which the real names were changed and the story was expanded into the lives of the former players.

I suggested that we write it together and just tell the story as it actually happened. Before I made up my mind on how to tackle this job, I spoke to some high school friends and got their opinions regarding the possibility of a book recounting the story of that game, and whether they thought it would be interesting enough to be a book. I asked a mutual lifetime friend, Schenectady attorney Ron DeAngelus, a 1953 Mont Pleasant High School graduate, about the idea. He replied, "If you can write the story and make it come out half as good as what really happened, it will be a best-seller." I also spoke to an old high school buddy, Lenny Dariano. I asked him if he remembered the unplayed game, and he answered, "Like it was yesterday." I think that was the moment I truly decided to tell the story.

As I conducted interviews with participants affected by the story, I heard the expression over and over again "like it was yesterday". I found the title for my book.

Mike and I began to research, but after a few months decided it was too difficult and time-consuming. We didn't have the literary expertise to do justice to the subject matter; so we put it on the back burner and just said, "Maybe later." Well, it's later.

In 2014 I found myself with an abundance of free time and started thinking once again about writing this book. I realized that if I didn't do it fairly soon, it would never get written, as the people who lived this story were not going to be around much longer. As it was, several people that I wanted to interview in 2007 were no longer alive, and their personal part of the story was lost forever. In addition, many of the people that *were* still around were forgetting the details, as their memories grew dimmer with each passing year. The story was about to fade away. So I dug up the previous research and started again.

Now I submit the story as I, and others, saw and remembered it; and I hope you get a fraction of the enjoyment from reading the story as I got from researching, writing, and living it.

Contents

Foreword

———•———

LIKE IT WAS YESTERDAY

MY IMMERSION IN THE ALL-ENVELOPING spirit of the traditional Election Day football game between Schenectady's Mont Pleasant and Nott Terrace high schools goes back a way. It was the three years, January '38-January '41, when I was a student at Mont Pleasant. In that era the aura of the approaching big game consumed the student body. There was an anticipatory excitement birthing a few weeks before the big day and surging to envelop the entire student body. Banners, corsages, and booster pin buttons sold big at the student store. A cheerleader assembly was called with the varsity introduced center stage. That our team might lose never entered our minds. The feelings that evolved brought the kids together as one. Today we call it a sense of community.

Fast forward the thirteen years from '41 to '54. One of the most rewarding happenings of my lifetime has occurred. I'll be the assistant principal at Mont Pleasant and then the principal over the years '54-'61. I'm delighted to find that the feelings appearing among the students by the approaching Election Day game are as high spirited, if not more so, as those of my early '40's days. I fall prey to the saying "It was like déjà vu all over again." How wonderful! This, despite these kids having grown up in the years when their nation was confronted by WWII and the Korean War.

There's an extra something about this November 1954 game. Both Pleasant's team and Terrace's team have had undefeated seasons to date. Wow, what a game it's gonna be! Nothing can keep the excitement down. That is, nothing that's normally acceptable. But the unacceptable, bordering on tragic, inserts itself. A Mont Pleasant player and one from Terrace have been stricken with polio. Polio, a dreaded disease of that era, was virtually eradicated by medical science a few years later. The risk of exposure by other team members loomed large, forcing the cancellation of that unparalleled Election Day game. There were no winners, only losers. Those whose loss was greatest were the boys confronting the inroads of polio.

Author, Dennis Bender, a Mont Pleasant freshman in '54, and now some 63 years older, turns out to have been most persevering in digging out the details of that extraordinary Pleasant-Terrace football season and, until this time, to have hidden his talents as an accomplished writer. Beyond his remarkable descriptions of all the games played that season by both teams, the author provides us with a worm's eye view of the sociological makeup and history, of two ethnic sections of 1950s Schenectady. Dennis brings the high and low points of the game that never was back to us "like it was yesterday."

From time to time educators get a bonus boost of satisfaction from the special accomplishments of a student with whom they've had school years contact. Thank you for the lift, Dennis. Those fortunate enough to have read this book will also be thanking its author.

Donald Sayles

CHAPTER 1

Schenectady

**You could bet on anything
in Schenectady.**

IN 1954, SCHENECTADY, NEW YORK, had a population of 92,000. It was a tough factory town.

The General Electric Company was founded in Schenectady in 1886 by Thomas A. Edison. The GE employed 35,000 people in their factories that made huge turbines, washing machines, radios, televisions, and just about any other electrical appliance for the home. It was a forerunner in the electrical industry, helping to meet the nation's and the world's growing electrical needs. Hardly anyone born in Schenectady ever left without at least a brief stint working at the GE or the American Locomotive Company, which was Schenectady's second largest employer. Schenectady's motto was "The City That Lights and Hauls the World".

Schenectady was known as a big gambling town with floating crap games, poker rooms in the back of newsrooms, numbers playing, horse betting, bookies and their runners—all highly illegal. Nobody seemed to care too much, not even the police. Some say Schenectady was a semi-Mafia town and that the newsroom owners and bookies paid protection to the vice squad. Gambling busts were few and far between and plenty of advance notice was given if a raid was scheduled. You could bet on anything in Schenectady... even high school football games.

Schenectady was more or less divided north to south by State Street. The main drag, lower State Street, held the downtown stores. There were three big department stores and four theaters, all on State Street. The north side of State Street was definitely the wealthier of the two sections. It held a huge city park called Central Park, which was built on the highest ground in the city. All the students who lived in the area north of State Street went to Schenectady's first high school, originally named Schenectady High School when it was built in 1903. The name was changed to Nott Terrace in 1931 when Mont Pleasant, the second high school in Schenectady, was built.

Schenectady High School was just on the edge of downtown and was a sturdy, two-story, gray brick building. A companion building and a walkway between the buildings was constructed in 1913, giving the school a capacity of about 1,000 students in grades ten, eleven, and twelve. Many of the students' fathers—most mothers didn't work outside the home in 1954—were in management at GE; many worked their way up through the ranks. By 1929–1930, the school could no longer accommodate the high school population for the entire city, so a new high school was built on the south side of town, about one-and-a-half miles from Schenectady High School.

This new school was on a hilltop in a mostly Italian and Polish working-class neighborhood called Mont Pleasant. The neighborhood of Mont Pleasant was on a flat to rolling plain, bound on the sides by deep ravines. On the western side was the Penn Central Railroad separating Mont Pleasant from Bellevue, and on the east, a ravine called the Hollow divided Mont Pleasant from Hamilton Hill. Broadway was the northern boundary, and the city line terminated Mont Pleasant from the south. The ravine was crossed by a high bridge known as Suicide Bridge. From the top of Hamilton Hill to the bottom of the ravine there was an 80-foot spiral walkway called Seven Heavens, down which kids would try to ride their bikes without hitting the brakes. It was impossible to do, but that didn't stop them from trying.

They named the new school Mont Pleasant High. It was a magnificent three-story red brick Colonial-style building situated on about 15 acres of land. Its charming quad, located in the middle of the school, had a lush lawn, trees, shrubs, walkways, and benches. It was cherished by both the students and faculty alike. The quad could be seen from every classroom that faced the interior of the school. The school was completed in 1931 at the cost of 1.2 million dollars, and immediately became the pride and joy of the entire neighborhood. Mont Pleasant had a student capacity of about 1,500 tenth, eleventh, and twelfth graders.

In the year 1954, Schenectady still only had the two high schools, so if you went to high school it was one or the other. You could actually choose which one you wanted to attend, Nott Terrace or Mont Pleasant. There was no busing except for the kids who lived way out of town on farms, so you had to get to school on your own; most students had to walk. The competition in all sports between these schools was fierce, and school loyalty lasted a lifetime. You attended the school closest to your home or you were labeled an outcast. The only people who would associate with you were the other "traitors". More of the kids in the Nott Terrace area decided to attend Mont Pleasant than the other way around. You rarely heard about anyone from the Mont Pleasant neighborhood going to Nott Terrace.

The football rivalry between these schools started in 1932 and continued until 1958, when Nott Terrace was replaced by a new, modern school closer to Central Park, named Linton. A new rivalry started immediately between Mont Pleasant and Linton; some said not quite as intense as the old rivalry, but a rivalry still. The fiercest rivalry was the football match between Mont Pleasant and Nott Terrace. It was a classic. It occurred on Election Day every year from 1932 to 1957, even through the Great Depression, World War II, and other difficult times. Every year, that is, except 1954.

Many interesting things were happening in 1954. The words "under God" were added to the Pledge of Allegiance. Swanson

& Sons introduced TV dinners. In Great Britain, the rationing that started during World War II finally ended. Joe DiMaggio, the superstar centerfielder for the New York Yankees, married Marilyn Monroe, one of Hollywood's hottest blonde stars. Schenectady was all abuzz about winning the Little League World Series. In the summer of 1954 the world was getting ready to discover the future King of Rock 'n Roll, Elvis Aaron Presley, from Memphis, Tennessee. A 19-year-old truck driver just out of high school, Elvis had just made history recording, *That's All Right*, a song that a 2004 *Rolling Stone Magazine* article argued was "the first rock and roll record".

Economically speaking, gas was 22 cents a gallon, a movie ticket was 70 cents. Minimum wage was 75 cents per hour, the average salary was $4,700 per year, and the average price of a new car was $1,700. The average home cost $10,250. Average rent per month was $85, and unemployment was 4.9% nationwide.

This was all very interesting, but nothing was more interesting to Schenectadians than the upcoming Election Day high school football rivalry game between Mont Pleasant and Nott Terrace. Nineteen-fifty-four was going to be a very special year. Since the rivalry had started in 1932, this was only the second time both teams were going to the fall classic undefeated. The first time it had happened was in 1941. This time, both teams were 5-0 and had played some common opponents, so everyone was scrambling to figure out who the odds-on favorite would be. That was important information in a town like Schenectady, where a small fortune was always wagered on the outcome.

CHAPTER 2

Crane Street

———•———

**You could get anything
on Crane Street.**

ON CRANE STREET IN MONT Pleasant there were three newsrooms
where you could get your bet down. A newsroom was an establish-
ment that sold newspapers, magazines, candy, and cigarettes in
the front of the store, while the back of the store was a gambling
operation, mainly numbers betting, poker, and other card games.
Crane Street sat right on top of Crane Street Hill and had about 40
stores in its own little neighborhood downtown. Here you could
get all of your needs and wants fulfilled within about five blocks
from end to end. The football coach at Mont Pleasant High School,
Larry Mulvaney, said, "Crane Street was great. We would play a
game on Friday night and then go shopping on Saturday and see
your players and a lot of fans doing their weekend shopping on
Crane Street." You could get anything on Crane Street, from fresh-
baked Italian bread, to fur coats, to your pick of two Greek diners
(just one block apart) where you could get several great meals for
about $1.50. The neighborhood had its own movie theatre, bank,
post office, hardware store, and four bars, in addition to every other
kind of store you could imagine. Crane Street also had its own beat
cop that all the kids knew and respected. Ray Zanta, whose barber
shop was next door to the post office, cut every Mont Pleasant guys
hair as well as some ladies. He would also sell prophylactics from

his back room to the high school boys who had enough nerve to ask him. Not that they ever got to use them; they just kept them in their wallets, where they left a permanent indentation, to show their friends how "cool" they were. Crane Street had everything.

Leading up to the rivalry game, emotions on both sides were running higher than usual. The taunting started early. One Mont Pleasant car full of fans sported a huge, hand-painted sign that read, "We are going to beat the 'Notts' off of Terrace." Pretty risqué stuff for 1954! You could get expelled from school for a stunt like that. Everyone was comparing player to player and looking for the edge. Mont Pleasant had a lightning-fast team with a hot-shot junior quarterback named Eddie Riccardi who could make you believe he had handed the ball off to one of his backs only to turn around with the ball still safely in his hands, firing a pinpoint pass to one of the ends already in the open. One of the huge problems with the Mont Pleasant team was that they were all small in stature—small, but tough. Eddie weighed in at 150 pounds.

The Blue-and-White of Nott Terrace versus the Red-and-White of Mont Pleasant rivalry was too big to be played at either school's football field. No siree, this classic was played at McNearney Stadium, which held 10,000—not enough seats for all the students and alumni that wanted to attended the game this year. For the first 20 years, the game had been played at Union College's Alexander Field; but in 1952 McNearney Stadium, with its newly lighted field, was offered for the games, even though the game was still being played in the afternoon, McNearney Stadium seemed a better fit. It provided a more neutral ground than Union College, which was firmly entrenched in Nott Terrace territory.

Union College was founded in 1795 as a private, non-denominational liberal arts college and was the first institution of higher learning chartered by the New York Board of Regents. The United States of America was only nine years old when Union started. For 175 years it was a traditional, all-male college, until 1970 when it began enrolling women.

At the time Union College was founded, Schenectady had fewer than 4,000 citizens and was in the middle of nowhere, the area being very nearly a wilderness. Union College has the distinction of having the longest-serving college or university president in the history of the United States—Eliphalet Nott served as president of the institution from 1804 to 1866, 62 years. Schenectady's first high school was later renamed Nott Terrace High School in honor of Eliphalet Nott. The city of Schenectady grew up around Union College. Once the commercial area started to develop closer to the Mohawk River, Union's 120-acre campus was right at the edge of the growing downtown. Schenectady had a college long before it had a high school, and it was Schenectady's pride and joy.

McNearney Stadium was erected in 1946 as the home of the Schenectady Blue Jays, a minor league baseball team affiliated with the Philadelphia Phillies. It was built by the McNearney brothers, Pete and Jim, who owned a nearby beer distribution company. Both Mont Pleasant and Nott Terrace started playing their home games at the stadium in 1952. A few years after the stadium's opening date, Jim and Pete had a feud. Jim McNearney slugged Minor League Director Joe Pearson over a dispute concerning Jim's habit of slipping his players a few extra bucks from time to time for an especially good game, which was against league rules.

Because of this altercation, Jim went back to the beer business and Pete took over the baseball team and stadium. The two brothers never spoke to each other again.

Since about 1953, attendance at minor league baseball games had been on a decline, attributed mostly to television's popularity. The Blue Jay ticket committee attempted to sell 2,000 season tickets at 25 dollars each in order to keep baseball in Schenectady. The deadline for the sale was December 31, 1956. When the committee reported that only 838 season tickets had been sold, Pete McNearney announced on January 2, 1957, that the Blue Jays were withdrawing from the Eastern League. After 11 years of operation in organized baseball, the team was folding.

Pete then built and operated a 9-hole golf course at the stadium's site; during the final baseball season the fans could actually see the work being completed on the golf course. The Stadium Golf Course was opened on July 10, 1958, and it integrated the grandstand shell into the clubhouse. The grandstand lights, seats, and bleachers were sold, and another piece of hallowed ground was gone forever. In 1965, Pete sold out to the Hennel family. They ran the 9-hole course and a pitch-and-putt course, leaving it until the 1970s, just as Pete had built it. Then they closed the pitch-and-putt and installed a driving range. Construction was then started on a new 18-hole course, which would not be completed until 1987; only two holes remained from the original course Pete McNearney had built. The Hennels still own and operate the course, which expanded to include a pro shop, a restaurant and bar, and a beautiful patio that overlooks the scenic ninth and eighteenth holes.

Many Schenectady companies gave their employees the whole day or a half day off on Election Day. Those football fans who did have to work either skipped out after lunch or called in sick in order to be at the game. Schools were let out at lunchtime. There was no bigger football rivalry game in Schenectady than the Mont Pleasant-Nott Terrace. If you had to choose between voting or going to the game, it was no contest.

But in order to make this even more interesting, let's hearken back to the 1953 match. Nott Terrace was undefeated going into the Election Day game that year, and Mont Pleasant had only one loss for the year. Mont Pleasant had lost its first game of the season to a perennial powerhouse from downstate, White Plains, the Westchester County champs. Nobody wanted to play this team. White Plains had not lost a game in four years and had an average winning margin of four touchdowns. They beat Mont Pleasant 12-0 in the bruising 1953 contest with no points being scored in the first half. Most of the teams in the state would have considered it almost a win just to *play* White Plains and be able to hold them to only twelve points. Mont Pleasant boys didn't have such disillusions;

to them it was a loss, and they wanted revenge. White Plains went on to remain undefeated for the rest of 1953 and owned a 35 game winning streak. Their first game in 1954 was scheduled with Mont Pleasant—more on that game later.

In the Election Day match of 1953, Nott Terrace beat Mont Pleasant 19-0. The real bad news for Mont Pleasant was that Nott Terrace's superb running fullback, Derry Cooke, was only a junior and was coming back to play the next year. In the '53 game Cooke scored on a 48-yard run in the first quarter, and Nott Terrace never looked back. Cooke shook off 4 Mont Pleasant tacklers before going the last 25 yards untouched for a 6-0 Nott Terrace lead. In a team meeting after that game, Nott Terrace's, Coach Pete Shulha, presented the game ball to Cooke for his outstanding performance on a team that Shulha called "the greatest team I ever coached". Derry Cooke was coming back as a senior—bigger, faster, and stronger.

CHAPTER 3

YMCA

———◆———

**Everybody pitched
in; Stan Fox made
sure of that.**

IN THE EARLY 1940s, THE estate of Mary Beckwith willed to the
YMCA its large, sturdy two-story stone home on a huge piece
of property in the Mont Pleasant neighborhood. The property
fronted Chrisler Avenue at the foot of Michigan Avenue and was
bordered by Lakeview Avenue on the West, Lower Crane Street on
the South, and Van Velsen Street on the East. There was a hill and
a wooded area behind the house and two large ponds stretched
out lengthwise, separated by an earthen bridge that was built well
enough for a car to drive over. Few, if any, YMCA branches anywhere in America could boast a property as unique as this 15-acre
piece of country in the city. The pond closest to the house was
used for a swimming hole, and the pond furthest from the house
was used for fishing in the summer, ice skating and hockey in the
winter. The YMCA boys would bring their snow shovels from home
and shovel while skating until the surface was as smooth as glass.

From the end of November until Christmas Eve the YMCA
sold Christmas trees as a yearly fundraiser. All of the YMCA boys
learned Salesmanship 101 while helping to sell, trim, and then tie
the trees onto their customers' cars. Everybody pitched in—Stan
Fox, the director, made sure of that; and the YMCA sold hundreds

of trees each year. If you lived in Mont Pleasant you bought your Christmas tree from the YMCA lot. After Christmas passed and everybody had taken down their trees, the boys would round them up from the neighborhoods around the YMCA well before the garbage collectors picked them up, and then they dragged them to the ice skating pond for a huge bonfire. The bonfire would finally put itself out when the burning pine trees had melted the ice. What wasn't burned crashed through the ice in a sizzling, smoking, spectacular climax– this to the rousing cheers of the assembled crowd.

There was an outdoor blacktop basketball court that was in constant use. In the summer, leagues were formed of high school and college players on summer break, and many former stars would play under the lights from 7:00 pm to 11:00 pm every weekday night. The league hired a timekeeper and a scorekeeper from amongst those boys who hung out at the YMCA. They were recommended by Stan Fox only if they were good kids and "kept their noses clean." Getting one of these jobs was a prized position as the league paid you four dollars a night. Four dollars was a lot of money for a young teenage boy in the 1950s. Stan Fox ran a tight ship and made it his business to know, on a very personal basis, every boy who hung out at the YMCA. Stan had a huge influence on the YMCA boys and kept many of them from doing anything too stupid, probably keeping quite a few out of jail in the process.

There were 10 cent movies and popcorn every Friday night during the school year, ping-pong tables, model building, sandlot baseball, football, and pick-up basketball games all day long. Some of the older boys would sneak off to play a card game for money – similar to blackjack; it was called seven-and-a-half. But if Stan got wind of it, the game didn't last too long. Same thing went for smoking. Stan rarely told your parents about any bad behavior; he just "handled" it himself. The way Stan "handled" kids who were out of line would probably get him sued and maybe even put in jail for child abuse these days, but things were different back then. Stan had a long paddle similar to a cricket bat – if you were his target

Frenchy's Hollow

for some infraction, all you usually heard was the "swoosh" of the paddle as Stan let you have it on your behind. In fact, if Stan disciplined a boy, that boy would never tell his parents for fear they would dish out a worse punishment at home. All the parents knew what a tough job Stan had with the YMCA boys and would stand behind him 110%.

The YMCA was just another part of Mont Pleasant that made the neighborhood boys as close as brothers. They learned to work as a team and to know what to expect from each other at an early age.

Ritchie Matousek lived on Lakeview Avenue in a house where the yard backed up to the YMCA property. He was one of the sand-lot football players who would have been on the Mont Pleasant team; but, unfortunately, in the ninth grade, he blew out his knee up at Frenchy's Hollow, a swimming hole about 8 miles outside of Schenectady on Route 20. Frenchy's Hollow was formed by the dam at Watervliet Reservoir and was located at the former site of a foundry and a grist mill. Its edges formed a deep ravine with an approximately 30- to 40-foot drop to the water; steep shale sides would cut your hands and feet while you were climbing the cliffs if you made the slightest slip. The property was private and had numerous posted signs, but the boys would sneak in and stay until they were caught and chased out. However, as soon as the guards would go on their way, the boys would sneak back.

Many of the boys who went out to Frenchy's Hollow hung out at the "Y" and were between 12 and 16 years old. You needed to be at least 12 years old to have built up enough nerve to ride out to Frenchy's on your bicycle, since the route was along a well-traveled state highway and was dangerous for bike riders. Nobody would *ever* tell their parents that they went out to Frenchy's. By 17 years of age, most of the boys had discovered cars and girls – much more exciting than long bike rides and a swimming hole. A large number of the 15 to 16 year old boys would swan dive off the cliffs from a height of about 20-25 feet. From the ground it didn't look so high; but once you climbed up there (and it was too late to turn around and go back), it was terrifying. As they started the climb, some of the boys (especially the younger ones) thought they could manage the dive, but then changed their minds at the top and jumped instead. Diving or jumping off those cliffs was another way for the boys to get to know each other, a rite of passage of sorts. Everybody remembered who dove and who jumped, who chickened out and who kept their nerve. The swan divers had the most nerve, and when it came time to choose sides for football, those guys were the first picks.

Often a group of boys would ride their bikes down to Frenchy's and spend the day swimming, diving, and playing King of the Rock, which is how Ritchie ended up injuring his knee. One boy pushed him one way and another pushed the other way while Ritchie was determined to stay on the rock as King. Goodbye knee, goodbye football. Although Ritchie couldn't play football in high school, he wanted to be a part of the team so he became one of the football managers during his 3 years at Mont Pleasant.

CHAPTER 4

Goose Hill

——◆——

If you were going to be in the neighborhood, you better be from the neighborhood.

THE BOYS WHO WENT TO Nott Terrace came from a wider geographical area than the boys who went to Mont Pleasant. The whole of Mont Pleasant was only 520 acres. The Nott Terrace boys attended one of three junior high schools, whereas almost all the boys who wound up at Mont Pleasant had attended McKinley Junior High School, which could be seen from the high school only a block away. A few also came from Van Corlear Junior High School from the Bellevue area. The Terrace boys either went to Central Park Junior High School, Oneida Junior High School, or Washington Irving Junior High School, which were all a fairly long walk from Nott Terrace. Because the boys from Nott Terrace came from these different schools, they didn't *know* each other in the same way as the boys from Mont Pleasant. Some thought this could make a difference in how well they played as a team and possibly in the final outcome of the game. Since the rivalry had begun, Mont Pleasant had won 13 games and Nott Terrace had won seven, with one tie game. But that sure hadn't made a difference in 1953 when Nott Terrace trounced Mont Pleasant 19-0.

The Nott Terrace boys came from the area north of State Street that stretched from one end of Schenectady to the other, from the poorer Stockade areas on the Mohawk River all the way to the ritzy upper Union Street area. But the core of the area, its heart and soul, was Goose Hill. Goose Hill got its name from the geese that were once raised in the neighborhood. A farmer named Fred Breek owned a house and barn on Van Vranken Avenue (at that time merely a dirt road) and raised livestock, including a large flock of geese. The geese would wander all over the hill up to Lenox Road; the residents started to call the neighborhood Goose Hill, and it stuck. Goose Hill's loose boundaries were Foster Avenue to the west, Salina Street to the north, Rosa Road to the east, and Nott Street to the south. Its main street was Van Vranken Avenue, and it was only a few blocks from Nott Terrace High School. The neighborhood was built in the early 1900s to house the American Locomotive Company workers whose factory was only a few blocks away. It consisted primarily of sturdy two-family homes occupied by mostly Polish and Italian families. These families produced tough little boys who went on to become even tougher football players in high school.

Not as well stocked with every type of store imaginable as Crane Street in Mont Pleasant, Van Vranken Avenue still had plenty of stores in which to buy all kinds of meats, vegetables, breads, beer, wine, and liquor—so basically, all the necessities of life. Perecca's Bakery made what many considered to be the best Italian bread in the world. No really, these people were *serious* about their bread. Perecca's was on Jay Street, a little bit of a walk from Goose Hill; but even though you could buy the bread in several corner stores on Goose Hill, it was worth the daily trip just to smell the aromas of that fresh baked bread direct from the bakery. Most loaves didn't make it all the way home without a corner being ripped off and gobbled up by the carrier.

Goose Hill was not blessed with a branch YMCA like the one in Mont Pleasant, but they had the 45-acre Steinmetz Park. Its pond and open field was where the boys and girls from the neighborhood congregated every summer from dawn 'til dusk. The pond was also the scene of daring midnight swims, at least until the cops caught the kids and chased them home. The city chlorinated the pond, and it had a floating dock on which you could work on your suntan or try to impress the girls with your cannonball skills.

Now, most of the boys who went to Nott Terrace High School might not have been as tight as the Mont Pleasant High School boys, but the boys from Goose Hill *were* tight…if not tighter. Sandlot football started early in life, and the boys played from early light until long after dark.

When Goose Hill was being built up in the early 1900s, many deeds had restrictions on who could purchase property in Schenectady and in what areas they could live. Polish and Italians could not buy property east of Van Vranken Avenue as they were considered second-class citizens by some and were not welcome in the more upscale neighborhoods. The houses built west of Van Vranken Avenue were simply constructed, but substantial, two-family homes for largely German and Irish skilled and white collar workers. In 1899 Union College sold the General Electric Company 90 acres of land just east of the college to pay off a debt. It was called the GE Realty Plot or just "The Plot". General Electric executives subdivided it and built homes on it with covenants requiring a minimum lot size and home value. There was no way the Goose Hill residents were going to be anywhere near this exclusive enclave. So, the streets west of Van Vranken Avenue and going down to the Mohawk River soon became dense with two-family homes.

But Goose Hill was to Goose Hillers their little kingdom—if you were going to be *in* the neighborhood, you had better be *from* the neighborhood.

CHAPTER 5

1954 Preseason

Nott Terrace Preseason

"Do it again."
-Pete Shulha

COACH PETE SHULHA, THE FORMER Manhattan College track and field star, who in 1954 was beginning his seventh year as head coach of Nott Terrace, had a problem—how to replace 12 first-stringers, including six from his front line. Shulha said, "How well we replace them will determine our success. You can't lose boys like guards Bob Czub and Pat LaPorta, ends Dick Stack and Chet Cavoli, center Al Prysmont, and tackle Ralph Buonome, and not feel it. We certainly won't have as much depth this season."

Last year's undefeated team, which had outscored its opponents 277 to 6, was playing almost the same schedule, and all of the teams would be out for revenge for the shellacking they had received the previous year. In 1953 the Downtowners of Nott Terrace had beaten LaSalle Institute 45-0; in the new season LaSalle was Terrace's first challenger—or victim, depending on your viewpoint.

Nott Terrace's Assistant Coach Chuck Abba was brought up in Mont Pleasant on Third Avenue, just a stone's throw from Crane Street. He was half Italian on his father's side and half German on his mother's side, so he fit perfectly into the neighborhood. He graduated from Mont Pleasant High in 1944. After a two-year stint in the Army Air Corps during World War II, he graduated from Union College in 1950 on the G.I. Bill. He was co-captain of his Union College football team. Abba went to work teaching history at Nott Terrace High from 1952 to 1955.

He was Pete Shulha's assistant football coach in charge of the linemen, as well as the game scout. A genuine dyed-in-the-wool Schenectady boy through and through.

Training in the new season had gone well, so far, for Shulha and his assistant coaches, Walt Przybylo, Roy Larson, and Abba. Shulha was more than pleased with his backfield prospects, despite the loss of quarterback Gomer Richards and halfbacks Tony Berry and Frank Elia. Coming back was senior Derry Cooke, the hardest-running fullback in county football the prior year, along with last year's second-stringers – quarterback Ed Wilgocki, and halfbacks Alonzo Burnham and Johnny Matarazzo. Nick Ronca, who had done well as fullback the previous year, was ready to play any position Shulha asked on either offense or defense.

This year's team promised to be more versatile than the 1953 team, which had mostly utilized a keep-it-on-the-ground, punishing, unrelenting assault. This year's team could go to the air from the T-formation with precision passing from Wilgocki. It could also use the double wing, with Cooke carrying the brunt of the attack on the single wing, and with Burnham and Matarazzo furnishing the speed that helped give Terrace so much depth in the 1953 season.

Along the line were starting ends Al Mangino and Willard Wiltse, both lettermen from the previous year. They were backed up by sophomores Jack Straight and George Kozak of the 1953 unbeaten freshmen team. Straight made the varsity team near the end of the 1953 season, showing considerable ability to catch the football. If Terrace decided to go to the air this year, he could be one of the starting ends.

Also up from last year's freshmen squad were Dave Jenkins, Larry Johanson, Bob Compachiaro, and Lou Visco, all vying for the positions held last year by Bob Czub (who was now playing at Cornell University) and Pat LaPorta—big shoes to fill for sure. At 205 pounds, returning star left tackle Johnny Bezio looked good again, along with Don Schermerhorn, who was weighing in at 200 pounds. Johnny Calvano and Hugh O'Connor were both trying to nail down one of the starting spots as tackle. Dick Kaczmarek, a 175 pound senior who played and saw substantial action last year, seemed to be Shulha's choice for center.

There were still more than two weeks to Game 1 against La Salle, but the stage looked close to being set for Terrace.

The Nott Terrace players were every bit as tough as the Mont Pleasant boys; and, like the Mont Pleasant boys, they took it out on each other. To win their starting position, they had to show what they were made of during scrimmages against their friends. Coach Shulha was a very strict coach, all business, all football. One of his familiar sayings, when he was not happy with his players' efforts, was "Do it again". Most of the players loved Shulha. During a three-and-a-half hour interview with Al Burnham, Al was asked, three different times, what he thought of Pete Shulha. Each time Al tried to answer he became very emotional to the point of not being able to speak. Finally, Al was able to manage, "He was like a father to me." And the subject was closed. But some also thought he was too tough, even brutal according to a few. Shulha was nicknamed "Black Pete" by some of the boys from the gym classes but was never called that by his loyal football players. In his second year of teaching at Nott Terrace, Don Sayles*, who was also the ski coach, remembers that some of his ski team also called Coach Shulha, "Black Pete". Sayles and Shulha were

---

* Sayles went on to become the assistant principal at Mont Pleasant High School in 1954 and then the principal in 1955. He also wrote the forward to this book.

ski buddies, and Sayles always thought Shulha "a great guy". One day when Sayles and Shulha were together in the school cafeteria, with others in hearing distance, Sayles asked Shulha how one of his highly publicized players could be playing football when he never went to classes. Sayles remembered what a suicidal thought that was to share with Shulha who was very angry with Sayles for his comment. On Valentine's Day in 1953, someone handmade a black heart Valentine's Day card and pinned it on the bulletin board just outside of Shulha's office. Coach Shulha wasn't fazed and went about his business without ever mentioning anything about the card.

During practices, center Dick Kaczmarek would need to be on his toes when centering to fullback Derry Cooke in the double-wing formation. If the ball wasn't perfect—right on Derry's knee—Derry would let him know about it. One day in practice while Kaczmarek was centering to point-after kicker Neil Golub (who went on to become Price Chopper's, a huge supermarket chain, CEO), an argument broke out between them about whether Dick had centered the ball badly or Neil had mishandled it. Words turned into deeds, and before you knew it, a fistfight ensued. It was broken up and both boys were running laps in the gym until Shulha felt they had cooled down enough. These boys were competitive and not afraid to say what was on their minds or to throw their fists. Then they would shake hands and get back to business. Dick Kaczmarek jokingly said in a later interview, "Maybe if I didn't have that fight with Neil Golub, I could have got a good job with Price Chopper."

Mont Pleasant Preseason

It didn't matter which side you were on, as long as you got to play.

Larry Mulvaney, born and raised in Springfield, Massachusetts, landed his first football head coaching position in 1952 at Mont Pleasant, and he was starting to understand just how close-knit these boys of his were. His high school football team was more of a neighborhood team; back in those days there was no organized football until you got to high school. (Pop Warner didn't come along in Schenectady until 1959.) But these boys had been playing sandlot football together since they could walk. They would simply choose sides and play from dawn to dusk – one day on this side, the next day on the other side. It didn't matter which side you were on as long as you got to play. They knew each other's strengths and weaknesses long before they ever put on the red-and-white jerseys of the Red Raiders. The boys knew better than anybody, coaches included, how tough each player was. One of the toughest was junior fullback Vince Gallo, a soft-spoken "A" student who had a Jekyll-and-Hyde personality. The quiet, polite young man turned ferocious when he put on his helmet; and for short-yardage plays, he was almost impossible to bring down. He was Mulvaney's kind of player and was almost guaranteed to play first string. Gallo could also kick field goals and extra points, a rarity in 1954.

The General Electric Company supplied equipment for both the Mechanical and Electrical Technical courses at Mont Pleasant. These courses consisted of mainly high level mathematics and were designed to find those students who excelled in math, and to interest them in engineering careers, hopefully to later work for the GE. The courses were very successful in doing both, but they didn't produce many football players—with the exception of Mickey Petrolle. The curricula required 2 extra classes per day, one at the end of the normal school day and one at the end of a shortened lunch break. Because of the extra class at the end of the day, Mickey came out for practice about an hour after the rest of the team. He missed warm-ups, calisthenics, wind sprints, running laps and the team meetings. He did not get to take part in the camaraderie of the team putting on their uniforms together, along with the joking, teasing, and harassing that went with it. It didn't seem to have any effect on Mickey's playing ability though. By the time he got onto the field, the team was already in serious practice mode. Mickey jumped right in with hardly a nod or a hello to anyone. This was the part of the practice he liked anyway—the hitting and the tackling. *Let's get down to business.*

Assistant Coach Tony Parisi, who was a letterman in both high school football and baseball, graduated from Mont Pleasant in 1950, then went on to Holy Cross where he was named an All-New England football player in 1953. After college graduation in 1954, he was back at Mont Pleasant teaching History and assisting Mulvaney on the sidelines. Parisi took a liking to senior fullback Danny Monaco (everybody liked Danny) and encouraged him to fight for a starting position. Danny had first encountered Tony at Hamilton Elementary School when Tony came to show his trophies to the class Danny attended with Tony's sister Dolores. Danny decided to make it his mission to be Coach Mulvaney's worst nightmare when the time came for a decision on whom to send in as the first-string fullback. Even though he knew Mulvaney was leaning towards Gallo to secure the position, Danny was not about to give up without a fight. He knew he had to be able to kick also, since Gallo was a clutch kicker. He started to practice all alone on the outdoor neighborhood YMCA basketball court. Kicking the ball from one end of the court to the other, he would then retrieve the ball and start over from the other side, doing this for hours on end. Lou DeMarco, left guard on the football team, who was a good friend of Danny's, observed Danny going through this routine day after day; and he told his friend he was sure he would be the No. 1 fullback on the team. If Danny wasn't going to start, it certainly would not be from his lack of trying.

CHAPTER 6

Game Week 1

Mont Pleasant vs. White Plains
Friday, September 24, 1954, 7:30 p.m.
Schenectady Stadium

"Don't look at their players."
– Larry Mulvaney

THERE WERE 1,200 MONT PLEASANT fans to greet the big line—and bigger reputation—team of White Plains when they came to Schenectady Stadium* football field. White Plains was a city just north of New York City with a population of about 45,000. They hadn't lost a football game since 1949; their winning streak was 35 games and counting. Their new head coach, Franklin Robinson, himself owned an 18- game winning streak with his former team from Rye, New York. He was looking to get a good start against Mont Pleasant, who had been beaten last year by the Plainsmen 12-0. Both teams shared a common locker room to get prepared for the game, and Head Coach Larry Mulvaney told his boys not to look at the players from White Plains for fear that they would be scared silly at the size of the White Plains line. The matchups on the line were almost comical in their comparisons:

---

* Schenectady Stadium was the official name, but most of the locals called it McNearney Stadium.

Mont Pleasant		White Plains
Larry Pivacek 5'11"/145 lbs	vs.	Ted Lee 6'2"/188 lbs
Joe Greene 5'10"/155 lbs	vs.	Stew Sesman 6'3"/205 lbs
John DiCocco 5'11"/175 lbs	vs.	Art Sheffer 6'4"/235 lbs
Bobby Patrick 5'9"/165 lbs	vs.	Chuck Deuterman 6'1"/ 206 lbs
Mickey Petrolle 5'9"/155 lbs	vs.	Sam Combriello 170 lbs
Joe Campisi 5'10"/180 lbs	vs.	Ralph Isley 196 lbs
Lou DeMarco 5'9"/175 lbs	vs.	George Wager 203 lbs

The Plainsmen line outweighed the Raiders line by an average of 35 pounds per man. Can you imagine battling with someone for 48 minutes who outweighs you by 35 pounds? The Mont Pleasant boys both *could* and *couldn't* wait for the action to start... what was wrong with these kids? The players from White Plains had never been on the losing end of a high school football game. Never. Not even once. Mont Pleasant's quarterback Eddie Riccardi, a junior who was starting his first varsity game, weighed in at 150 pounds and wore thick glasses; but he could hide a football from the defense, until he was ready to let it fly, better than any high school quarterback around. In a 2007 interview Coach Mulvaney commented that Eddie was the best ball handler he had coached in his entire career. It was Mulvaney's first game with this bunch of first-string players; and if he still didn't quite realize just how tough of a team he had, he would by the end of the game. Nobody was going to scare these kids, no matter how big they looked or talked. The Mont Pleasant boys were of the opinion that the bigger they are the harder they fall, and they would be proven correct tonight.

With the Mont Pleasant band blaring their fight song, "Victory March" (made famous at Notre Dame), the teams came to midfield for the start of the game. White Plains won the coin toss for opening kickoff but had to punt after three plays and an offside penalty. Taking the ball from their own 24-yard line, Mont Pleasant took 13 grinding plays to hit pay dirt. Vince Gallo took it in over from the two-yard line for a 6-0 score, and the Red Raiders never looked back.

Then Mickey Ferraro—who all the Mont Pleasant girls thought was a dead ringer for movie star Tony Curtis—intercepted a pass to bring the ball to the White Plains 18-yard line.

Then Eddie Riccardi threw it a little short, but Mickey still gathered it in and picked up blocking to go the rest of the distance...12-0.

Eddie Riccardi was only a junior and not as closely knit in as the senior members of the team. He was soft-spoken and maybe a little gentler than most of his teammates. Mickey Petrolle, who was one of the toughest and oldest players on the team, whispered to Eddie after the first play that Mickey was going to have no trouble with his opposing player on the White Plains line and that Eddie could "run over him all day." Petrolle, who had a keen mind and a deep insight into the game, tried to give Eddie tips during the game whenever he saw something that could give Mont Pleasant an advantage. Back in those days quarterbacks called their own plays and had to make adjustments as the game progressed. This was Eddie's first varsity start. When Eddie signed Mickey's yearbook at the end of the school year he wrote, "I will never forget the help you gave me in the White Plains game." These guys were truly a team and didn't mind sharing the glory, as long as they won.

By this point, White Plains was getting nervous and starting to panic, fumbling on their own 25-yard line. Mont Pleasant recovered; and on the third play from scrimmage, Carmen DiVietro went wide left and scored. Eighteen-zero with just minutes left in the first half.

White Plains' halfback's lateral went awry in the second half kickoff, and this time a whole host of Mont Pleasant players, led by Mickey Petrolle, recovered on the 23-yard line of White Plains.

Mont Pleasant's running backs took turns racing the ball to the 10-yard line, and then Mickey Ferraro covered the remaining distance by cutting back inside the right tackle. Vince Gallo scored the extra point, making the final score 25-0. White Plains' winning streak was over. The game even got reported in the New York Times, the reporter misspelling Mont Pleasant (calling it *Mount* Pleasant) when he asked, "Who do these guys think they are?"

As the White Plains team was getting ready to leave, Danny Monaco went onto their bus to return an umbrella someone had left in the locker room. One of the players asked him, "What's wrong with you guys, are you crazy or what?", referring to the ferocious and sometimes vicious tackling and blocking that the Mont Pleasant boys executed play after play with no let-up, even when the game was well put away.

A few years later a scandal developed in White Plains when it was revealed that the school had actively recruited potential football stars living outside the school district, even to the point of paying the parents' expenses to move to White Plains.

Louie DeMarco and Mickey Petrolle couldn't wait for the city papers to come out on Saturday. They had been best friends since grade school and had been having fistfights since third grade, both being fierce competitors. But even though they fought against each other, pity the poor soul who dared to say anything bad about one of them, or tried to pick a fight with one of them. *They* could beat up each other, but nobody else better try. They always competed to see who would receive the most mentions in the newspaper account of the football games. Mickey's father was Frankie Petrolle, a popular former boxing celebrity and local bar owner; so whenever Mickey was mentioned in the press, "son of Frankie" was tagged on either before or after his name. The nickname stuck with his teammates, although mostly said behind Mickey's back.

During the White Plains game, for the first time, Coach Mulvaney saw with his own eyes how tough these players were and how well they understood each other when it came to the game of football. Yeah, he had seen them play some last year, but mostly as reserve players. Even watching them at practice had not prepared him – he now saw them in a whole new light. When the chips were down, he was astonished at what they could do.

Nott Terrace vs. LaSalle Institute
Saturday, September 25, 1954, 7:30 p.m.
Hawkins Stadium

Any thoughts of LaSalle winning were over in less than a minute.

LaSalle Institute was a private, all-male Catholic preparatory school for grades six through twelve located in nearby Troy, New York. It had been established in 1850 by the Brothers of the Christian Schools.

The Cadets of LaSalle Institute, with a 7-1 record last year, their only loss being to Nott Terrace, had 11 returning letterman and revenge on their minds. Terrace had beaten LaSalle the previous year 45-0, and it didn't take long to crush any thoughts of the Cadets ending Nott Terrace's winning streak of seven straight – less than a minute, in fact.

Nott Terrace was sizzling hot for the first half with touchdowns from fullback Derry Cooke on an up-the-middle 63-yard romp and an 80-yard inside reverse from halfback Alonzo Burnham. Fullback Nick Ronca steamed nine yards for the second touchdown of the night. Tackle Johnny Bezio plunged in for the point after. Then, with only seconds left in the first half, quarterback Ed Wilgocki straightened up from the T-formation to hit Al Mangino for a 10-yard scoring pass. That's all they needed, and that's all they got. Terrace did not score in the second half, leaving some wondering if they had enough stamina and talent to defend their undefeated performance from last year. LaSalle scored with four minutes to go in the second half for a final score of 25-7. The touchdown didn't prove much except that Terrace *could* be scored upon.

Offensively, Alonzo Burnham carried the ball eight times, picking up 164 yards, and caught two passes for another 37 yards. Defensively, the 5'10", 165-pound terror tackled viciously in his linebacker role and covered his territory like a blanket. Alonzo won the Schenectady Gazette's Athlete of the Week award for the week of September 25.

CHAPTER 7

Game Week 2

———

Nott Terrace vs. Amsterdam
Friday, October 1, 1954, 7:30 p.m.
Schenectady Stadium

**Already thinking
about the Election
Day game**

AMSTERDAM, WHO HAD BEATEN THEIR archrival Gloversville High the previous week and had their best-looking team in years, had high hopes at the start of this game. Twenty-five hundred fans turned out. It was the top Friday night high school football attendance since the games had moved to Schenectady Stadium two years prior. Amsterdam, which had plenty of fans on the sidelines, following the kickoff, made four straight first-downs, most of the yardage on quick openings from the T-formation. Then their wheels came off. Nick Ronca and Al Mangino made key tackles, and Terrace took over on their own 27-yard line. Derry Cooke opened up the middle and never looked back. Three plays later Derry scored, then he plunged in for the extra point. Nott Terrace, 7-0. Four plays later Nott Terrace center Dick Kaczmarek scored again after blocking a punt and taking it in from the 17-yard line. Nick Ronca roared over for the extra point just as the first quarter whistle blew. Two more touchdowns and an extra point in the second quarter made it 27-0 at halftime.

Derry Cooke took the second half kickoff to midfield before being brought down, then galloped 13 more yards to the Amsterdam 37-yard line. Alonzo Burnham took it the rest of the way on a reverse from the double wing. Minutes later Alonzo scored again. Tackle Johnny Bezio went into the backfield to add the extra point of rushing.

Coach Pete Shulha took mercy (sort of) and sent in the second and third teams for the rest of the game. The Terrace players scored twice more for a final score of 53-0. The Amsterdam players were happy to see the end of this game. Amsterdam had to face Mont Pleasant in two weeks, which would give the football betters and bookies the first chance to get a comparative score on a team both Mont Pleasant and Nott Terrace had played. Everybody was already thinking ahead to Election Day.

Mont Pleasant vs. Albany High
Saturday, October 2, 1954, 2:00 p.m.
Hawkins Stadium

Danny's only touchdown

In their first game, the previous week, Albany had beaten rival Philip Schuyler 20 to 6. They were probably dreaming about the Class A title for this year, if they could only get by Mont Pleasant. No way!

Hawkins Stadium was located in Menands, a suburb of Albany, New York. It is about halfway between Albany and Troy. In 1928 Hawkins Stadium was built to become the home of the Albany Senators, an Eastern League baseball team. In 1930, the General Electric Company in Schenectady installed lights for the night games. The stadium was right next door to Mid-City Park which had a roller coaster, roller skating rink, merry-go-round, and swimming pool. Back in the 1930's, this was considered an exciting entertainment complex for the whole family. In 1931 the New York

Yankees played the Albany Senators in an exhibition game held at Hawkins Stadium before a crowd of 6,300, with Babe Ruth hitting two home runs. The Senators played their home games there until they folded in 1959. The stadium was then sold to pay back taxes and razed in 1960. Albany and Troy High Schools and LaSalle Institute all played their home football games at Hawkins Stadium.

The field at Hawkins Stadium was rain drenched, so the Eddie Riccardi-led Red Raiders turned cautious and kept the razzle-dazzle to a minimum on the muddy gridiron. The sun had broken through after a 2-hour midday rain, and the weather was ideal; but the field was still so muddy that any subs that came into the game were immediately recognized by their unsoiled uniforms. They didn't stay clean for long. In the first quarter Carmen DiVietro took a Riccardi pitch and ran it 45 yards for Mont Pleasant's first touchdown. Before his first quarter was out, Mickey Ferraro showed the Albany defenders the number on the back of his jersey as he grabbed a pitch-out, cut wide, and completely outdistanced the Albany High Garnet's secondary on a 65-yard touchdown gallop. Score, 12-0.

A Riccardi-to-fellow-junior-Joe-Green pass, good for 20 yards, set up the third touchdown with the completion moving the ball to Albany's three-yard line. Ferraro knifed through to the one-yard line, and then co-captain fullback Danny Monaco dived over for the touchdown. This would be the only touchdown that Danny scored in his senior year at Mont Pleasant.

Albany tried filling the air with passes, but the Raider's defense held up and most of the Garnet tosses were batted down or fell short. Albany heaved up passes while the Raiders, playing it cool and cautious, threw only six, hitting on two of them. They were content just grinding it out in the mud. The first drive-and-score in the second half came after Mickey Ferraro, who had a power-fully-built lower torso, dashed for 45 yards. This set up a Larry Pivacek grab of a wobbly aerial thrown by Riccardi into the end zone for a 17-yard touchdown. Coach Mulvaney explained that

Ferraro was nicknamed "Steel Legs" by the team because he just shook off tackles in the open field and could hardly be brought down once he got a bit of steam going.

Mont Pleasant scored eight touchdowns in their first two games, but only two extra points, pointing out a weakness in a team otherwise showing no wrinkles in offense or defense. It would take them a few more weeks to solve that problem; but solve it, they would.

This win was Mont Pleasant's first Class A Conference win and marked the second week they had won with a 25-0 score.

CHAPTER 8

Game Week 3

Mont Pleasant vs. Newburgh Free Academy
Friday, October 8, 1954, 7:30 p.m.
Schenectady Stadium

The "Marvel" meets his match.

NEWBURGH GOT TO THE GAME a little late; and before the evening was over, probably wished they had never gotten there at all. Newburgh came into the game 1-1 for the year; they lost their first game to Greenwich, Connecticut, 45-7, and won their second game the prior Saturday against their archrival Poughkeepsie High, 13-7. Their bench strength was reported as being weak; and if that was true, their first-stringers were in for a long, rough night. First-string quarterback Bill Huber, halfback Paul Benosky, and end Mickey Burkowski were the stars on the team, but that's about all they had. Heaven help them if Mont Pleasant really got going.

About 2,000 fans showed up at Schenectady Stadium. As the night got started, in the first quarter, Mickey Petrolle recovered a fumble on the Mont Pleasant 23-yard line to stop a Newburgh threat. Then in three running plays, which included a terrific midfield block by Lou DeMarco, the combination of Carmen DiVietro, Mickey Ferraro, and Danny Monaco got the ball to the 47-yard line. Mickey Ferraro went on a 50-yard tear to Newburgh Free Academy's three-yard line, then took it the rest of the way to the end zone for a 6-0 lead. Newburgh Free Academy's next effort got stopped short at Mont Pleasant's 14-yard line, and DiVietro and Ferraro had long runs of 34 yards, 22 yards, and a final 28-yard left-end run to the end zone by DiVietro...12-0. Mont Pleasant was still having a hard time scoring extra points and, in fact, had only scored two in ten tries. Nobody had ever scored a point against Mont Pleasant so far this season, so it didn't seem to matter too much. Four plays later Ferraro scooped up a Newburgh Free Academy fumble and raced into the end zone for his second touchdown of the evening. Eddie Riccardi hit end Joe Green for the point after (*finally*) for a score of 19-0 at the half.

Newburgh put together four first downs at the start of the third quarter, advancing the ball all the way to Mont Pleasant's 12-yard line. Mickey Burkowski* (nicknamed "The Marvel" by his team-mates) grabbed in a 15-yard pass, but Mickey Petrolle rolled a flying tackle under him, stopping his advance on the spot. Burkowski was sent to the sidelines with an elbow injury that didn't appear to be too serious, but kept him out for the rest of the game. Then on third down Lou DeMarco made a big tackle which forced Newburgh Free Academy to go for it on fourth down. The entire Mont Pleasant line rushed the Newburgh quarterback for a 9-yard loss and Mont Pleasant took over the ball on downs. Then steel-legged Mickey Ferraro was almost caught in the backfield but got loose for a 7-yard gain. On the next play, Mickey took the ball off tackle and gained 66 yards, with Vince Gallo blocking the last Newburgh tacklers at the Academy's 15-yard line, to give Mickey his third touchdown of the night. Vince plunged over for the extra point to make the score 26-0. Coach Mulvaney started to send in some reserves to finish the game. Mickey Ferraro intercepted a pass on the Newburgh 25-yard line, then Vince Gallo went right up the middle for 23 yards to the two-yard line where Vince Savini,

---

* Burkowski who went on to become NFA's J.V. basketball coach for five years and varsity basketball coach for 19 years, had a varsity record of 260-70.

second-string junior halfback, took it in for the game's final touchdown. Final Score: Mont Pleasant-32, Newburgh Free Academy-0. Another shutout, three in a row.

For the first three games of the season Mont Pleasant had rushed for 749 yards and passed for 83 yards, compared to their opponents' tally of 286 rushing yards and 165 passing yards. Mont Pleasant's speed and Eddie Riccardi's excellent ball-handling made for some tremendous running plays and tons of yardage gained. Next up: Amsterdam, whom Nott Terrace had beaten badly two weeks ago with a score of 53-0. This would be a good comparison game to determine if either team had an edge on the other. The next week Nott Terrace was playing Newburgh Free Academy, so maybe by the following weekend everyone would arrive at a clear favorite for the Election Day rivalry.

Nott Terrace vs. Troy
Friday, October 8, 1954, 7:30 p.m.
Hawkins Stadium

Sonny scores.

Nott Terrace put its nine-game winning streak on the line on a cold autumn evening against the Flying Horses of Troy High School on their home turf. Here we go again. One minute into the game Alonzo Burnham recovered a fumble on Troy's 15-yard line; and one minute later on the second play from scrimmage, the hard-hitting halfback was in the end zone...6-0. The next time Terrace got the ball, on the third play of the series, fullback Derry Cooke dashed 70 yards for a touchdown. Nick Ronca scored the extra point on a slant play.

Before the game clock showed ten minutes gone, the Blue Devils scored again, after blocking a punt on Troy's 32 yard line. Two plays later quarterback Ed Wilgocki hit Alonzo in the end zone. Derry plowed through the line for the extra point. Could any team stop the Alonzo Burnham and Derry Cooke duo? Probably not—unless Mont Pleasant came up with a plan, and they definitely were already working on one.

In the second quarter Nick Ronca intercepted a pass on Troy's 21-yard line and carried it down to the 13-yard line. Enter Derry Cooke, two plays later—touchdown, and to top it off, he ran the extra point in too. Troy had the ball for one play before Nick Ronca grabbed a stray pass and took it to the five-yard line before being hauled down. John Matarazzo got one yard on the first play. Enter Alonzo Burnham—touchdown. Thirty-three to zero at the half.

Four plays after the second half kickoff, Alonzo, after getting a great block from end Jack Straight, raced for 57 yards deep into Troy territory. Time to bring in the subs to let them get some playing experience. Another fumble by Troy, then five plays later, second-string halfback Dick DeSarbo put six more points on the scoreboard, going in from 12 yards out. Derry scored the extra point... 46-0.

Troy Coach Ed Picken's boys still hung in there; with quarterback Kent Duncan firing away, the boys from Troy got over the 50-yard line for the second time in the game. Kent then flipped one to his end, Charlie Walker, getting all the way to the Nott Terrace 8-yard line. Terrace stiffened, but on fourth-and-goal Kent hit end Denny Stone to finally get on the scoreboard and avoid a shutout. In Nott Terrace's first three games, this was only the second touchdown scored against them. Halfback Lou Marchese plunged over for the extra point...46-7.

The two Blue Devils, Alonzo and Derry, teamed up on the next set of downs to score again. Alonzo picked up the first nine yards needed, and then Derry took it 78 yards in just two plays. Could any team stop these two?

Fourth quarter—everybody knew this game was over. Alonzo had scored four touchdowns, Derry three. Coach Picken was going to let some of his second-stringers get playing time too. Troy quarterback John Muth got lucky—although he missed his intended receiver, the errant ball dropped right into the hands of Denny Stone near midfield, and he just kept running for his second touchdown of the game.

Not to be outdone, Terrace second stringers came back with one more score. Junior third- string halfback Sonny DeVito broke loose for 28 yards and a touchdown. It was the only touchdown Sonny would ever score with the Blue Devil varsity team. Final score, 58-14.

Nott Terrace only allowed Troy 44 yards on the ground while amassing 464 yards in their own ground-chewing game. Next up for Terrace-downstate Newburgh Free Academy on Saturday in an away game.

The Downtowners were starting to say it aloud: *Nobody can beat us. Bring on Mont Pleasant.* And the chant went up, "*Kill the hill! Kill the hill!*"* over and over again.

---

* "Kill the Hill" was a reference to Mont Pleasant High School.

CHAPTER 9

Game Week 4

—■—

Mont Pleasant vs. Amsterdam
Friday, October 15, 1954, 7:30 p.m.
Schenectady Stadium

Hurricane Hazel

THE AMSTERDAM TARZANS WERE COMING back to Schenectady Stadium, where two weeks ago they were mauled by Nott Terrace, 53-0. To prove a point, the boys from Mont Pleasant wanted to beat them even worse this week and get bragging rights over Nott Terrace.

After slamming into Haiti on October 12 and leaving between 400 to 1,000 dead, Hurricane Hazel, a Category 4 hurricane, made landfall in the United States at the North Carolina-South Carolina border. On the morning of October 15, Hazel battered the coastline with 150 mile per hour winds. A storm surge of 19 feet almost completely wiped out Garden City, South Carolina. By 7:00 p.m. the hurricane was over Pennsylvania and central New York, clocking sustained winds of 75 miles per hour and gusts of over 90 miles per hour. Hurricane Hazel was the deadliest and costliest storm of the 1954 hurricane season. Nice night for a football game. Hurricane Hazel was blowing through the area, and it was pouring down rain before the kickoff. There were only about 700 fans at the stadium, including four busloads that bravely came down from Amsterdam. It had stopped raining just before kickoff, but the wind was blowing mightily. Amsterdam had to play with the wind in their faces in the first quarter; and before the first quarter was over, the game was too—for Amsterdam at least. Mont Pleasant led 28-0. Mont Pleasant threw only one pass in the entire penalty-plagued game with Mont Pleasant being penalized 85 yards and Amsterdam 80 yards. Amsterdam's quarterback Ralph Matalf was injured in the first quarter and had to be taken to Schenectady's St. Clare Hospital with a broken rib. Mont Pleasant scored a total of eight extra points—five by Vince Gallo—and sent all the sportswriters scrambling to the record books to see if any team had ever come close to accomplishing this feat.

Only two good things happened to Amsterdam all night, and one of them occurred at halftime. Amsterdam brought a 96-piece marching band and 40 cheerleaders and majorettes with them for the best halftime show ever seen at Schenectady Stadium. They formed a heart with an arrow through it while swaying back and forth to "Heart of My Heart". Even the Mont Pleasant fans cheered wildly during the show.

Meanwhile, in the Mont Pleasant locker room with the halftime score 42-0, Sig Makofski, the administrative director of sports for Mont Pleasant, told Coach Mulvaney to let up a little and get the game over with, since the rough weather was showing no signs of stopping.

The referees told both coaches that they were going to speed the game up. Mont Pleasant's team manager, freshman Sid DiMascio, was struck near the eyebrow when high winds blew a metal down-marker sign out of the ground. Sid had to get a few stitches along his eyebrow, but this was the only serious injury on the Mont Pleasant side.

Coach Mulvaney was using mostly subs in the second half and played every boy on the bench. Amsterdam's backbone got stiff in the fourth quarter against Mont Pleasant reserves, and they pulled off five first-downs to get to the Mont Pleasant seven-yard line. Mont Pleasant first stringers were begging Coach Mulvaney to put them back in for a goal line defense to keep their shutout record for the year going. Mulvaney sent the first-string line back in, but in a driving rain and sea of mud, Amsterdam's fullback Stan Piurowski faked out Mont Pleasant co-captain Lou DeMarco for a five-yard plunge and a touchdown. This was the second good thing that happened to Amsterdam all night. These were to be the only points that would be scored against Mont Pleasant all year. Mickey Petrolle would never let his grade school rival, Lou DeMarco, forget (in a friendly, ribbing kind of way) who they went over in order to score them. Mont Pleasant scored eight touchdowns: one by Eddie Riccardi on a quarterback sneak; three by Mickey Ferraro rushing; one by Larry Pivacek on a fumble recovery and a 17-yard scamp to the end zone; one by junior Vince Savini, a second-string halfback, on a 40 yard run; and two by third-string fullback Peter von Rogov, both by rushing—the first a 16-yard end run and the second a six-yard plunge up the middle. Mont Pleasant won 56-6; the previous week Nott Terrace had beaten Amsterdam 53-0. The bookies were still all shaking their heads—it didn't look like there was going to be a clear favorite.

Nott Terrace vs. Newburgh Free Academy
Saturday, October 16, 1954, 1:00 p.m.
Newburgh

"Kill the Hill."

Nott Terrace was taking on NFA, who had just played Mont Pleasant the week before and had been beaten up by the Raiders, 32-0. This game would be a good comparison between Mont Pleasant and Nott Terrace. Terrace was also bringing their ten-game winning streak with them to Newburgh.

There was no scoring in the first quarter for either team. Terrace marched 51 yards for a second quarter touchdown, Alonzo Burnham getting the drive going with a 32-yard run to the

Newburgh 19-yard line. John Matarazzo and Alonzo got it to the nine-yard line, and then on the third down, Matarazzo took it over for a 6-0 lead. Cooke ran the extra point over for a 7-0 lead that they took into the locker room at halftime.

Midway through the third quarter, NFA's Mickey Burkowski— whom Mickey Petrolle had thought he had taken out for the season with a spectacular tackle the previous week— grabbed a Bill Huber aerial for a 52-yard touchdown pass, but Terrace blocked the extra point kick to escape being tied...7-6 Terrace.

This was way too close for comfort for the Terrace boys, but then Derry Cooke took the ensuing kickoff 89 yards and went all the way to the end zone. Then Johnny Matarazzo scored his second touchdown of the day when Newburgh fumbled the Terrace kickoff. Terrace scored again with an Ed Wilgocki-to-Alonzo Burnham touchdown pass. The final score was Nott Terrace 32, Newburgh 6. Eleven straight wins for Nott Terrace. Next up for Terrace was Gloversville on Friday night at Schenectady Stadium, then bring on Mont Pleasant. *Kill the Hill* was heard again.

CHAPTER 10

Game Week 5

—•—

Nott Terrace vs. Gloversville Friday
October 22, 1954, 7:30 p.m.
Schenectady Stadium

**"That bunch of
farmers."
-Al Burnham**

THERE WAS JUST THIS ONE last game before Nott Terrace was going
to really get down to business.

Nobody expected Gloversville to be anything more than a
warm-up game for Nott Terrace before the big Election Day game
against Mont Pleasant. Terrace's 11-game winning streak was
surely not going to be broken by Gloversville. No way.

Thirty-two miles west of Schenectady lay the small city of
Gloversville, population 23,000. When ladies wore gloves, from
about 1890 to 1950, 90% of all the gloves sold in America were
handmade in Gloversville or its nearby sister city, Johnstown. There
were over two hundred glove factories between the two cities.
Schenectady people always considered the folks from Gloversville
to be sort of farmers. It was kind of an insult, like "that bunch of
farmers", but Al Burnham knew that the boys from Gloversville
were a rough, tough bunch of farmers that always gave Nott Terrace
trouble on the football field. They did in 1954 for sure.

Gloversville's tight 5-4-2 defense almost completely subdued Nott Terrace's usually potent double-wing offense. Nott Terrace offense could not figure out what the Gloversville linebackers were going to do next. Good thing for Terrace that they had a defense too, or this could have been the end of their winning streak.

Nott Terrace scored a pair of safeties, the first one when a high pass from center forced punter Don Houghton to step out of the end zone in the first quarter. Then in the second quarter Johnny Bezio nailed Jim Izzo behind the goal for the second safety. Ed Wilgocki hit Alonzo Burnham in the first quarter for a touchdown. Gloversville defense scored in the first quarter when Nott Terrace fullback Nick Ronca slid off the left side for what looked like a five-yard gain, but the ball got jarred loose right into the hands of a surprised Houghton; who then, escorted by the entire Gloversville line, dashed 65 yards for a touchdown. Halftime score 11-6, Nott Terrace. Let's skip over to Hawkins Field and see how Mont Pleasant is fairing against Troy.

Mont Pleasant vs. Troy
Friday, October 22, 1954, 7:30 p.m.
Hawkins Field

Sweet play! We are going to try to burn Alonzo Burnham with it.

Mont Pleasant was playing their last game before meeting Nott Terrace in the Election Day game, and this would be the last chance to compare teams that both played this year. Nott Terrace had played Troy on the same field two weeks ago and had walloped them 58-14. Troy had scored more points against the Devils than any other team this year, but Nott Terrace in return scored a year-high of 58 points against Troy. The bookies needed *something* to help them calculate the point spread. Surely, *this* would be that game.

Troy proved to be an easy win for the Red Raiders of Mont Pleasant. The final score was 33-0, and if it wasn't for a season-high of 97 yards in penalties* and an 80 yard touchdown-run-after-interception by Mickey Petrolle being nullified because he stepped out of bounds at Troy's 45-yard line, the final tally for Mont Pleasant would have been in the 50s at least. The halftime score was Mont Pleasant-26, Troy-0.

In what was probably Joe Green's best game all season, both he and Mickey Ferraro each had two touchdowns. Halfback Carmen DiVietro also got one. Joe Green picked up a fumble in Troy's backfield and went in from Troy's 15-yard line for his first touchdown. In a play that Mont Pleasant would probably try to use against Nott Terrace in the Election Day game, Eddie Riccardi pitched out to Mickey Ferraro, who then tossed a 36-yarder to left end Joe Green, who, in turn, took it 40 yards untouched to the end zone. Sweet play! It was a play that Coach Mulvaney was going to attempt again to burn Nott Terrace's Alonzo Burnham. It worked against Troy beautifully, but he wondered if the experienced and savvy Burnham would fall for it. Time would tell.

At halftime the news that Nott Terrace was struggling in their game against Gloversville spread like wildfire through the stadium. Terrace was only up 11-6. Mont Pleasant was taking care of business with Troy to uphold their end of the unspoken agreement with Nott Terrace to come into the Election Day game undefeated, and Terrace better come through too. All of the coaches, players, and fans for Mont Pleasant were rooting for Terrace to put Gloversville away in the second half. Nobody at Mont Pleasant

---

* This year's record 97 penalty yards the Mont Pleasant team racked up was due to revenge the players were trying to exact on the Troy players. At last year's Troy-Mont Pleasant game, the Mont Pleasant bus was late arriving for the start of the game. Troy's Coach Picken insisted they start on time. Mont Pleasant Coach Mulvaney was concerned that some of his boys might suffer injuries due to the lack of game prep. Bad blood ensued. Thus the 97 pay back penalty yards.

wanted Nott Terrace to lose a game yet – if anyone was going to beat Terrace and stop their two-year-long winning streak, it was going to be Mont Pleasant. This was long before cell phones and instant communication, so word of the game results didn't filter down to the folks at Hawkins Stadium until the Mont Pleasant game was almost over. Terrace prevailed 25-6. Phew! Nothing was left between now and Election Day except practice and strategy sessions for both teams with no more chances to figure out who was the better team. Everyone would have to wait for game time. This would not be settled anywhere except on the gridiron.

CHAPTER 11

Game Week 6

———•———

Mont Pleasant vs. Nott Terrace

Their pride was almost as big as Tony's thighs.

TONY PARISI, MULVANEY'S ASSISTANT COACH and the backfield coach, who had just graduated the year before from Holy Cross and had four years of college football experience, liked to practice with the boys and was still extremely competitive. While getting ready for the Terrace game, he set up a scenario where he pretended to be Nott Terrace star fullback Derry Cooke; the ball would be centered directly to Tony, and he would take off into the line depending on where he told his blockers he wanted to go. Tony, who weighed at least 250 pounds, was huge compared to the Mont Pleasant players. Initially, he didn't wear any pads or a helmet because he didn't think he needed them to get by the defenders, but he was in for a surprise for two reasons: one, the boys on the line were not afraid of anybody, and their pride was almost as big as Tony's thighs; and two, one of Tony's blockers, a tough freshman named Chubby Pantalone, was tipping off the defenders as to which way Tony was going to run. Tony (who did not like to be called by his real first name *Benzo,* although all the boys referred to him as Benzo behind his back) tried again and again to break through the line to no avail. Benzo was stopped in his tracks.

The next day Tony came out to practice wearing his old Holy Cross helmet, and, with informant Chubby Pantalone relegated to the sidelines, started to run through the line almost at will. Coach Mulvaney saw what was going on and called an end to it before somebody ended up getting really hurt. Tony had proven his point but so had the linemen of Mont Pleasant – they were not afraid of anybody.

CHAPTER 12

Danny

Danny Monaco, age 18

Danny was going to be a Marine. That was settled.

EVERYBODY CALLED HIM DANNY. EVERYBODY liked him. He didn't have a mean bone in his body. He was born into an Italian-American family in 1936 in Schenectady. From an early age he was missing some family structure in his life. His parents had divorced when Danny was in the fifth grade, and he had been largely self-reliant since then. Danny was tall and athletic, with a boyish-yet-brooding look and a "better than Elvis" hairdo. At times, he had a somewhat dark and melancholy expression; but whenever he was around friends, his big, bright smile broke through. Throughout the course of high school, he lived with various relatives, sometimes sleeping on a friend's couch when he wasn't staying with his grandmother, uncle, and a cousin in a three-room flat on Lafayette Street in downtown Schenectady. His uncle slept on the couch and Danny on a rollaway bed.

Danny could have easily decided to go to Nott Terrace High School when he lived with his grandmother; the school was just a few blocks from her flat, but he never even gave it a thought. Danny grew up in Mont Pleasant, and Mont Pleasant was his only choice for high school. Mont Pleasant was about 1½ miles from his grandmother's downtown flat; the bus ride cost only 10 cents, but Danny was very careful with any money that came his way and walked both ways. If Danny didn't go right home after school, he usually wound up at the YMCA. If he didn't get an invite to a friend's house for supper, he got a salami sandwich on Italian bread and a soda from the small corner store across the street from the Y and hung around alone until the guys came back after they ate their dinners at home.

Between his junior and senior year of high school, Danny, Ritchie Matousek, and another friend named Eddie Green joined the Marine Corps Reserve and traveled to Camp Lejeune in North Carolina for two weeks of basic training. The training mostly consisted of understanding military protocol, learning how to march and salute, getting into physical shape, and learning how to clean a rifle. During this time, Danny's main source of income was the pay he received from participating in these Marine Corps drills. The three friends were headed for a four-year enlistment once they graduated from high school. After basic training was completed, the boys would then be attending once-a-month meetings in Schenectady until they graduated from high school and began their enlistment.

Danny was just an average student and wasn't that interested in studying. In fact, he really didn't have a comfortable place to study even if he wanted to—no room in a three-room flat and nobody encouraging him to hit the books. No thought of college, since there was no money anyway. Danny was going to be a Marine. That was settled.

When football practice started in September, Danny was determined to be the first-string fullback even though the competition (in the name of Vince Gallo) was fierce. Vince was one of Coach Mulvaney's favorites, and he was a runner who could hardly be brought down in short-yardage situations. But Danny was a senior, and most of the other players on the first team were also seniors, and Danny's lifelong pals. This year was it for Danny—his last chance to play high school football. Vince was a junior and could have his turn next year as far as Danny was concerned. When Mulvaney named the first team, Danny was his starting fullback. Danny and senior guard and good friend Lou DeMarco were named co-captains by their teammates. Mont Pleasant was ready for the games to begin.

CHAPTER 13

Sonny

————

**"My boy just lived
to play in the Election Day Game."
-Charles DeVito**

HIS GIVEN NAME WAS OLIVER DeVito, but everybody called him Sonny. Sonny was born in a neighborhood midway between Nott Terrace and Mont Pleasant High Schools. The oldest of four siblings, he had two brothers and one sister. From a young age, Sonny was interested in sports, and football was his love. He attended Washington Irving Junior High School, and his dream was to go to Notre Dame and play football there. Sonny was short,0 but powerfully built, with close-cut dark hair and horn-rimmed eyeglasses that gave him a studious look. He was quiet and shy, sometimes seeming even a little aloof.

By the time he got to Nott Terrace, he had decided he was going to be a fullback. Sonny's dad, Charles, said, "Sports meant more to my son than anyone could realize. He played basketball...at the Jewish Community Center League, caught in American Legion baseball for Post 1005, and generally was in some kind of sport from one end of the year to the other." His father also said, "My boy just lived to play in the Election Day game. You know what this game means to the kids. He talked about it morning, afternoon, and night. He was only a second stringer, but he never doubted he'd play, and he felt he'd do himself and his friends proud." Outside of football, cars—fast cars—were Sonny's passion from an early age. He worked at a service station while he was attending high school and could not wait until he saved up enough money to buy his first car. It was going to be much longer than he ever could have imagined.

CHAPTER 14

Polio

———————

Why couldn't they find a cure?

POLIO. THE WORD JUST KIND of rolls off your tongue; if you didn't know what it meant and had to guess you might think it was a delicious Italian dessert or some new board game. But in the early 1950s the mere mention of the word struck fear into the hearts and minds of all who heard it, especially parents of young children. In those times every headache or sore neck a youngster complained of had mothers thinking in the back of their minds, *could it be polio?* Not knowing how the disease was contracted or prevented, combined with the knowledge that polio had no cure—and *still* doesn't—made this dreaded disease all the more frightening. While there were other diseases that were killing far more people per year (for example, influenza), the fact that polio's origin was unknown and that it usually struck the young and active contributed to its menace. In addition, some of these other conditions did not have the lifelong ramifications associated with paralytic poliomyelitis. Because of the ambiguity regarding its transmission, people were left helpless - holding their breath, crossing their fingers, saying a prayer.

Polio is short for poliomyelitis, which is now known to be a viral infection. The name *Poliomyelitis* derives from the Greek *polio* meaning grey, *myelin* referring to the spinal cord, and *-itis* denoting inflammation. It had been around for thousands of years, but nobody was really aware of the scope of its devastation until the 20th century. Ironically, it was not until the improved sanitary conditions of that century that polio became a serious threat. Polio is a virus that is transmitted via the fecal-oral—or less commonly oral-oral—route; for centuries, infants were routinely exposed to minute quantities of the virus due to the unsanitary living conditions of the time, such as open sewers or contaminated food and water supplies. Because the majority of the population was naturally immunized to the virus in infancy, when the risk for paralysis was low, it resulted in a disease that was relatively mild and uncommon. Once people no longer had this natural immunity, the disease took on epidemic proportions; and as the average age of the victims rose, so did the severity of its effects.

In 1921 at the age of 39, Franklin Delano Roosevelt, who was to become our president in 1932, contracted polio and was left with severe paralysis. In this pre-vaccine era, the specter of polio became like a living entity—watching, waiting, and then striking indiscriminately. If a man on the path to the presidency could contract polio, then it could strike anyone. Paralytic poliomyelitis, the type that Roosevelt had, only affected 0.1-0.5 percent of all the people who contract the disease. The paralytic type was very rare in small children—out of all persons who contracted polio, a young child would have a one-out-of-a-thousand chance of getting this type. On the other hand, the paralytic form of polio struck one out of every 75 *adults* who were diagnosed with polio. In addition, the extent of the paralysis increased as the age of onset increased. In the 1950s, the peak age incidence of paralytic polio was five to nine years, but one-third of the cases were reported in people over 15 years old. Although the initial onset of the disease typically lasted only a few days, the devastating results of this form of polio were permanent. Patients were left coping with these residual after effects for the rest of their lives. Sadly, this was the type of polio that was headed to forever alter the lives of two Schenectady boys.

In 1924 Roosevelt traveled to Warm Springs, Georgia, and checked into a cottage on the grounds of the dilapidated Meriwether Inn because of reports that the water there could somehow cure paralysis. Two years later he purchased the Meriwether Inn, and the Warm Springs Foundation was formed. Unfortunately, even though the warm springs felt soothing to polio sufferers, they offered no cure.

Then in 1934 there was a major outbreak of polio in Los Angeles. Nearly 2,500 cases were treated within a nine-month period in L.A. County General Hospital alone. One year later, physicians Maurice Brodie and John Kolmer competed against each other, each trying to be the first to develop a successful polio vaccine. Their field tests failed with disastrous results, as the vaccines were blamed for causing many cases of polio, some even fatal.

President Roosevelt announced the creation of the National Foundation for Infantile Paralysis (another name for polio) in 1937. Roosevelt and his law partner Basil O'Connor created the lay-governed organization based on grassroots fundraising and volunteer effort. The next year, the wildly popular entertainer Eddie Cantor coined the name "March of Dimes" as he urged radio listeners to send their spare change to the White House to be used by the foundation in the fight against polio. There were coin canisters on the counters of just about every local bar and corner store all across America; and everybody, including little kids, would chip in with their change to help fight this dreaded disease. During the showing of double feature movies, the movie would be stopped, the lights would be turned on, and the ushers would pass canisters around for donations. The name stuck, and the March of Dimes continues today.

An informally-trained Australian bush nurse named Elizabeth Kenny had developed a new treatment for polio; she traveled to Los Angeles, California, to demonstrate her methods, but was largely ignored by the medical community. She decided to take her treatment protocol to the Mayo Clinic in Rochester, Minnesota, where she gave her first presentation in the United States, to members of the clinic's staff. Her treatments consisted mainly of applying hot packs to and performing exercise on the affected limbs. Within the next four years she had started the Sister Kenny* Institute, and her procedures become the standard treatment for polio patients in the U.S., replacing all other methods of treating polio, which had been shown to be ineffective.

However, while the treatment offered some relief to the patients, it again was not a cure. Even so, Sister Kenny's methods are credited with being the basis for modern day rehabilitation treatment.

After the Second World War ended in 1945, 20,000 cases per year of polio were reported for each of the next four years, qualifying it as a full-blown epidemic. The fear created by this looming, malevolent presence was palpable. *Why couldn't they find a cure?*

In 1947, Dr. Jonas Salk accepted a position at the University of Pittsburgh's new medical laboratory founded by the Sarah Mellon Scientific Foundation. He set his sights on a vaccine that would work to prevent polio. Salk's laboratory was one of four awarded research grants for the polio virus typing project. He decided to use the newly developed tissue-culture method of cultivating and working with the polio virus that had been developed by Nobel Laureate John Enders at Harvard University. Other researchers, including Dr. Albert Sabin, who would later develop the oral polio vaccine, continued to do their work with monkeys infected with the polio virus, a more difficult and time-consuming process. Nineteen fifty-two brought the worst year of polio ever in the U.S., as 58,000 were stricken with the disease and more than 3,000 deaths reported. Polio's reign of terror continued, biding its time as it gained momentum. The need for a preventive vaccine was at a level of desperation.

---

* In 1919 Kenny earned the title of Sister, which in the Australian Army Nurse Corps is the equivalent of a First Lieutenant.

Early versions of the Salk vaccine, using killed polio virus, were used successfully with small samples of patients at the Watson Home for Crippled Children and the Polk State School, a Pennsylvania facility for individuals with mental disabilities. The next year, amid continued polio hysteria, there were 35,000 cases of polio in the U.S. The epidemic was showing no signs of abating; so, ready or not, the vaccine would need to be implemented. Massive field trials of the Salk vaccine were sponsored by the National Foundation of Infantile Paralysis, mostly being administered to younger children. Across the United States, 623,972 school children were injected with the vaccine or a placebo, and more than a million others participated as observed controls. The results, announced in 1955, showed promising statistical evidence that Jonas Salk's killed virus vaccine was 80-90 percent effective in preventing paralytic poliomyelitis.

But the success of the vaccination came too late to help two young men – one from Mont Pleasant and one from Nott Terrace. The thread connecting these boys? The epic rivalry between their two schools. And, against astronomical odds, the insidious force called polio was about to wreak devastation on the lives of Danny Monaco and Sonny DeVito within days of each other.

CHAPTER 15

Tragedy

———

**Saturday morning, October
30, 1954, and the teams
woke up to a cold, dreary
day.**

ALL THE ATTENTION HAD BEEN on Mont Pleasant's first game against downstate perennial powerhouse White Plains. The Plainsmen had not lost a game in five years and had beaten Mont Pleasant the year before 12-0. White Plains struck fear into the hearts of their opponents; nobody wanted to play them. But Mont Pleasant had whipped them 25-0; and so, with four games still to play before the Terrace game they started thinking ahead to Election Day. Everyone knew you were supposed to take the games one at a time and not start looking ahead, but the Raiders knew how good of a team they were and really had no fear of the other teams on the schedule before they played Nott Terrace. They easily won their next four games, outscoring their opponents 146-6, using mostly second- and third-stringers in the second half. Danny Monaco and Vince Gallo rotated in and out of the fullback position with plenty of action for both. Danny only scored one touchdown during his senior year.

Not only the players, but also everybody in town was thinking about Election Day. As the season went on it became apparent that no team could even come close to beating either Mont Pleasant or

Nott Terrace. The Election Day match was shaping up to be the biggest and best game ever of their 22-year rivalry.

Mickey Petrolle had the top down on his 1952 Pontiac convertible and was cruising down California Avenue on a beautiful autumn day with three of his teammates, Bobby Patrick, Mickey Ferraro, and Louie DeMarco. All four of those boys in the car would go on to become All-County Football selections. That year they were the backbone of the team, no question about it. All were enjoying the scenery, but three of them, Bobby, Louie, and driver Mickey Petrolle, were also enjoying a big *no-no* for Mont Pleasant football players—a cigarette. Coming from the opposite direction in his car was Mont Pleasant baseball coach, Larry Eschen. Coach Eschen saw the boys smoking and reported it to Coach Mulvaney. Coach Eschen wasn't positive who had been smoking, or who exactly was in the car, but was sure he knew, at least, one of the boys was smoking. Mulvaney called Mickey Ferraro into his office and not-so-gently put Mickey up to the wall and loudly grilled him on who had been smoking. Mickey swore he hadn't smoked (which was true) but would not spill the beans on who had. Mulvaney tossed Mickey out of his office with a vow to get to the bottom of the matter. One of the team rules was that if you got caught smoking you were off the team, so Mulvaney knew he had a dilemma on his hands. The four boys came up with a plan to keep themselves on the team. Louie DeMarco had a younger brother Tony (whom everybody called Goo-Goo) who was a junior and also on the football team. In two passing cars they looked enough alike to be mistaken for each other, so the boys talked Tony into going to Mulvaney and confessing that he had been the boy Coach Eschen saw smoking. Coach Mulvaney bought the story, and the whole thing blew over, to the great relief of everyone involved—except Tony DeMarco, who got bounced off the team for the rest of the season. Talk about brotherly love.

Neither Mont Pleasant nor Nott Terrace had a weekend game before the Tuesday Election Day game, but both teams had scheduled weekend practices, Mont Pleasant even arranging one for Sunday. Coach Mulvaney had scheduled a light practice for Saturday morning, October 30, and the team woke up to a cold, dreary day. When the coach got to the school, some of the assistant coaches and players had already arrived. Danny and senior center Joe Campisi had met at Joe's house, about halfway between Danny's grandmother's house and Mont Pleasant High School, and had walked in the rain to the practice, getting drenched in the process. Mulvaney was walking down the school corridor to the gym office when he noticed some glass and a broken picture frame on the floor. When he reached the gym he asked what the hell had happened, and one of his players told him it had been an accident—Danny had started to slip; and when he grabbed the wall to break his fall, he accidentally pulled the picture down. Nobody was hurt, and after the coach said *okay,* nobody thought another thing about it, at least not for a while.

Danny had a sore ankle from the incident, so before the practice Coach Mulvaney was taping his ankle. Danny complained about a stiff neck, and Mulvaney told him maybe he slept on it wrong. The practice got started, but shortly after Danny complained of a piercing headache and began throwing up. Mulvaney told him to hit the shower and get ready for a television appearance that was a regular feature of the pregame at that time. Jim Poirer, one of only two freshmen on the varsity team, helped Danny into the locker room. Danny wanted to go home but felt so sick that he knew he could not walk to his house, so he uncharacteristically called his father to pick him up. As soon as he saw Danny, his father knew something was wrong. The other players on the team who saw Danny thought so too. The family physician, Dr. Richards, made a house call and diagnosed polio almost immediately. They took Danny to St. Clare Hospital, and the doctors there ordered a spinal tap. Once the doctors saw the spinal fluid, the chilling diagnosis of polio was confirmed without question. The color of the fluid was grey, the literal meaning of the Greek word *polio*. Danny was immediately transferred to City Hospital and placed in isolation.

Tony Parisi, who was a big fan of Danny's, was the first one up to the hospital, then Coach Mulvaney and Co-captain Lou DeMarco saw Danny. Mulvaney received a call at home about 1:30 that afternoon from Dr. Richards and was told that Danny was a sick boy. The doctor asked Mulvaney not to tell anyone that Danny had polio, as the one thing they didn't need was panic.

On Sunday morning when the players showed up for practice, Mulvaney sent them home without an explanation; however, people were starting to figure out what was wrong, and the rumors were running rampant.

And then, inconceivably, a day later catastrophe struck again. This time to one of Nott Terrace's own. During the week before the Mont Pleasant game, Coach Shulha had been on Sonny's DeVito's case for not putting out like he normally did. Then at a practice at Union College football field that same week, Sonny had felt a pain in his back; he thought he had just gotten hit the wrong way, so he cut the practice short. A slight limp developed, which Sonny thought was surely only a temporary nuisance. But on Halloween night, October 31, the pain became so unbearable that he was taken to City Hospital where they performed a barrage of tests. The gut-wrenching diagnosis- polio. Just like that, Sonny's season was over, along with all his hopes and dreams for the future.

The timeline of the events was unthinkable—first, a Mont Pleasant player, then a day later a Nott Terrace player, mere days before the culmination of their teams' joint rivalry. At 7:00 that same Sunday evening, two days before the game was scheduled to take place, an announcement was made on the local radio station that the Election Day rivalry game was being postponed. Initially, the game was simply postponed; then later that same day, it was canceled due to fear of the highly contagious level of the dreaded disease. The possibility of someone else falling victim to polio while at the game was too great of a risk.

As sick as he felt on the morning of the Saturday practice, in his mind Danny was still determined not to miss the long-anticipated game. But his determination was no match for polio; he *did* miss it, and so did everyone else—players and fans alike—who had been charged up to settle this 22-year-old rivalry. This unplayed game, and the unfinished rivalry that it represented, would forever haunt these two teams, and many of the people of Schenectady as well.

When viewed from the perspective of the catastrophe that befell Danny Monaco and Sonny DeVito that October, the cancellation of the game was trivial. But the canceled match became symbolic of something far more significant—in the minds of the people, it would forever be intertwined with the tragedy of these two vibrant, young men being struck down in the prime of their lives. Because of that, it became so much more than just a game. For the young people in the community, especially the players, it represented a coming-of-age moment—the comprehension that they were not invincible, and that bad things happened to good people. For the adults, it was their worst fears realized brought to life in a close-to-home tragedy.

CHAPTER 16

Coping

——————

"My legs wouldn't work."
-Sonny DeVito

IN THE WEEKS AND MONTHS that followed these devastating events, the town of Schenectady and the surrounding communities rallied around the two boys, trying to raise money to combat the disease that had toppled two of their own. Programs printed for the cancelled football game between Mont Pleasant and Nott Terrace would be sold on State Street by 20 students, ten from Mont Pleasant and ten from Nott Terrace. The program's marked price was ten cents, but people could donate any amount they wished. The proceeds went to a special polio fund. Fans who already held tickets for the game were encouraged to donate their refunds to the fund-raising drive; and most, if not all, did.

Danny and Sonny had known each other casually. They saw each other around but didn't hang out or ever even talk to one another. That was about to change. Their shared misfortune was about to make them more than mere acquaintances. After both had contracted polio within a day of each other that autumn of 1954, they ended up in adjacent beds in the same isolation room at City Hospital. As they faced the reality of their situations, the boys feared for their futures. They saw other patients in the iron lung and in braces, and they were scared. The first time Danny had a suspicion that he was going to be paralyzed was when Sonny fell off the bed in their shared room and told Danny to call the nurses for help. After the nurses got Sonny back into the bed, Danny asked him why he hadn't just gotten back in bed himself. When Sonny told him, "My legs wouldn't work," Danny thought, "If Sonny's legs don't work, maybe mine don't either." But Danny made a conscious decision to fight it with everything he had.

The young men remained in isolation for two weeks, playing checkers to pass some of the time. Then the Sister Kenny method of therapeutic treatment for polio began, which involved the application of hot packs and required them to remain completely still while lying on their backs. They would have to remain in this position for hours; to be able to eat they needed to be fed by hospital volunteers. During the time together, one of the boys' many visitors was pitcher Bob Feller of the Cleveland Indians, who autographed baseballs for Danny and Sonny. Feller had been in town to speak at the Mont Pleasant Athletic Club dinner.

After about four months Dr. Richards, Danny's first doctor, persuaded him to go to Sunnyview Hospital where he believed the treatment was better. Sunnyview, however, was much more restrictive—visiting hours were fewer and shorter. Sonny remained at City Hospital.

Six months after the polio struck, Danny received a muscle transplant. He then began taking his high school classes with a school district teacher who was assigned to teach all grade levels at Sunnyview. Danny was determined to be sitting up on the stage at Mont Pleasant for his graduation ceremony. He was convinced that he was going to fully recover and would be able to walk again. His friend Ritchie Matousek was a regular visitor, along with Ritchie's girlfriend, Mary Jane Scirocco. During one sneak visit, Danny held up his new braces for Ritchie to see from across the room. Danny saw the expression of shock on Ritchie's face as he came to the realization that Danny was going to have to wear braces. Ritchie, who had fully expected Danny to be out of the hospital by this time, finally understood the seriousness and permanence of Danny's condition.

Mary Jane, a Mont Pleasant senior cheerleader and a life-long friend of Danny's, met him in the third grade at Hamilton Elementary School. After his diagnosis she became one of his most frequent visitors at Sunnyview Hospital, sometimes even staying after hours. She recalls one late night visit when she somehow managed to get up on the roof of the hospital and climb through a window in order to see Danny.

George DeCarlo, another Hamilton School lifelong friend, recalls seeing Danny in an iron lung, "a big, brown thing that had air rushing through it with just Danny's head sticking out." George, who everybody called Choch, was one of the boys who hung around the YMCA and was always ready for a pick-up football game. All the sandlot boys thought that when they got to high school Choch would be their quarterback, but during a sports physical, the school doctor discovered that Choch had a hernia – that was the end of his football dreams. His mother said there was no way she was going to let him risk further injury, and that was it.

George got the job as freshman football manager to remain involved with his friends on the team; however, his career was short-lived after some of the older boys on the team bamboozled him, within a two-week period, into handing out the whole years' supply of nice, white wool socks and rolls and rolls of white tape. Needless to say, Coach Mulvaney fired him.

At first everyone was trying to stay positive, hoping and praying for a full recovery for both boys; but it was not to be. Sonny realized that at the tender age of 17 his football days were over, and it was a bitter pill for him to swallow. Because Danny had some respiratory problems, initially his case was considered the more serious. He was transferred to Sunnyview Hospital for rehabilitative treatment, and Sonny was eventually released from the hospital and sent home. Sonny was very dispirited for a while and was, in his mind, hopelessly confined to the wheelchair, while Danny was able to walk with the help of braces. Sonny soon realized he did not want to waste away doing nothing. Instead of going back to Nott Terrace, where the stairs were steep, he went to Mont Pleasant, going on to graduate in 1957, only one year later than his classmates. Danny graduated in 1955, on time with the class he started with.

CHAPTER 17

All-County Football Team

—————

**Just the eleven boys who
were the best**

BACK IN THE FIFTIES, EVERY player on the team didn't get a trophy
at the end of the season just for participating. Back then there
were still *winners* and *losers*, sometimes causing feelings to be hurt.
Every year the Schenectady newspaper, the *Union-Star,* named an
All-County football team of the 11 best players in the county. No
second or third teams, no runners-up, no made-up honorable
mentions—just the 11 boys in the county who were the *best.*

In 1954 all 11 players came from only two teams: Mont Pleasant
and Nott Terrace. There were two other high schools in the county,
Draper and Scotia; but in 1954 they didn't count for much in
regards to football. Mont Pleasant and Nott Terrace dominated the
county football scene, and everybody knew it. Four of the players,
Derry Cooke, Al Burnham, and Johnny Bezio from Nott Terrace,
and Mickey Ferraro from Mont Pleasant, were the top selections
for All County. Cooke and Bezio from the 1953 All-County Team
were almost sure to repeat,

Derry Cooke, co-captain of the Blue Devils, was a vicious,
straight-ahead runner who could go all the way from anywhere on
the field. Playing from the fullback position out of a double wing,
Derry generated almost unbelievable speed, scoring 64 points with
nine touchdowns and ten extra points. When Derry was called

upon to pass the ball, he threw for better than a 50% completion rate. Punting was another skill for the versatile senior, with four of his 50-yarders going out-of-bounds inside the opponent's ten-yard line. Derry could do it all.

Alonzo Burnham, the other co-captain of the Nott Terrace team, claimed the right halfback position in the All-County competition. Alonzo scored 54 points on nine touchdowns, many on long runs into the end zone. He also called the plays, rocked opponents with bone-jarring tackles, and played both offense and defense. Al was the rallying point for the Terrace players.

Mickey Ferraro, Mont Pleasant's halfback, was the county's top scorer with 66 points on 11 touchdowns. Scoring on runs of over 50 yards was the rule rather than the exception for "Steel Legs".

Johnny Bezio was Nott Terrace's left tackle and the biggest player on the All-County Team at 6'1", 220 pounds. Playing both offense and defense, Bezio was fast enough to be called upon for some point-after attempts in a line-smacking role.

Bobby Patrick, Mont Pleasant's right tackle, was consistent all season long with speed for downfield blocking. He was a perfect example of the take-charge attitude displayed by the fast- charging Raider line.

Larry Pivacek, Mont Pleasant's left end, was the lightest player on the All-County Team at 5'11" and 145 pounds. Despite this he blocked well and was a threat to go all the way on every pass completion.

Joe Green, Mont Pleasant's right end and the only junior on the All-County Team, was a very capable defensive player who didn't look back once he caught a pass, but kept his eye on the end zone.

Mickey Petrolle, Mont Pleasant's right guard, made tackles all over the field. He had a true team spirit and was the Raiders' fastest lineman. Mickey played both ways, commonly obliterating opposing ends and linebackers. He had half a dozen interceptions in the 1954 football season.

Lou DeMarco, Mont Pleasant's left guard, complemented Petrolle perfectly. Friends since elementary school, they knew each other so well that often a wink or a nod was all that was necessary to redirect a play or call a blitz. DeMarco played both offense and defense.

Dick Kaczmarek, Nott Terrace center, was a standout on defense who played with great poise.

Ed Wilgocki, Nott Terrace quarterback, was Mr. Versatility- a blocker in the double wing and a precision passer. He was ready and able to run or punt in any situation.

The 1954 All-County Eleven was a team keynoted by speed and a more explosive scoring punch than any of its predecessors. Many would agree that this team was the best Schenectady All-County Team ever.

As all were seniors, except Joe Green, and because of the polio scare that prompted the cancellation of the annual Nott Terrace-Mont Pleasant Election Day game, no one would ever know how they matched up against each other on the gridiron. That said, no one could doubt that these eleven players were the ones to watch if the game had been played.

When reading nonfiction books or watching movies based on true events, people often hope that the author or screenwriter will include a section that tells what happened to the principal characters later in life, especially if they were young. Usually it's a section in the back of the book, or in the final credits once the movie is over. There is rarely, if ever, enough information given to satisfy one's curiosity. For those who feel the same way, this section is provided to answer any lingering questions you might have: "I wonder what happened to..."

DERRY COOKE

Derry was one of the lucky ones on the 1954 Nott Terrace football team – his football career was not over with the cancelled Election

Day game. Derry got a full football scholarship to Lafayette College in Eastern Pennsylvania, but because of an injury to his thumb when it was caught in a saw while building an addition on his grandmother's house, he didn't get to play until the last five minutes of his college freshman year. In those last five minutes, he gained more yards than his entire team had in the first fifty-five minutes of that game. Derry did not return to Lafayette College for his sophomore year because he felt that the coach was not interested in him. He came back to his hometown of Schenectady and worked for the next two years on a road gang with the AFL-CIO. Derry then went back to school at Parsons College in Fairfield, Iowa, where he met his future wife and received his Bachelor of Science degree. Derry attended Clarkson College in Potsdam, New York, from which he received his Doctorate in Chemistry in 1963. Following graduation, he then did research at Clarkson for 15 years. For four to five years, Derry worked on the Lord Rayleigh Theory of Scattered Light and proved the theory to be correct. After leaving Clarkson's employment, Derry returned to school for two-and-half years to receive his electrical engineering degree in 1981. He made a career with Reynolds Metals in Potsdam for 18 years before retiring.

Derry and his wife, Margaret, have a daughter, Suzanne, and have totally embraced the hunting and fishing culture of northern New York State, where they still reside.

Alonzo Burnham

The head basketball coach at Nott Terrace, Walt Przybylo, helped Al get a full athletic scholarship to American International College in Springfield, Massachusetts, where Al only stayed for one semester before deciding college was not for him. He returned to Schenectady and worked as a civil servant for the state in Albany. In 1957, Al had the opportunity to play for the Brooklyn Dodgers; his tryout was with the Albany Black Sox, an all-black team, and he made the team as catcher. He was the only white player on the team and played just two games before being moved to a Double A Club in Macon, Georgia, called the Macon Dodgers. Al played with them for two years. In 1958 he married his first wife, Marlene. Then in 1959, Al was hired by the Schenectady Police Force and made sergeant in 1975. He was in charge of the vice squad from the early 1980s until his retirement in 1990, completing an exemplary career of 31 years. Al raced stock cars from 1954 to 1972 and was a regular driver at White's Beach Speedway.

In 1969, when Al was 32 years old, the *Capitol* newspaper sponsored an outdoor show at the Schenectady Armory. One of the attractions was Victor the Wrestling Bear; and anyone who was brave enough could battle with Victor, who was seven feet tall and weighed around 400 pounds. Al stepped up and after several minutes managed to maneuver Victor with a move he had learned wrestling at Nott Terrace High School, pinning Victor to the mat. Al was one of the few challengers to ever pin the bear.

Al had three children, Mark, Robin, and Amy, with his first wife. He has been married to his second wife, Lois for 34 years. They spend the winter living in Clearwater, Florida, and the summer living in Rotterdam, New York. When Al is in Schenectady, he meets on the second Wednesday of every month at Peter Pause Restaurant across from Union College for breakfast with some of his former football team members.

MICKEY FERRARO

After graduation from Mont Pleasant, Mickey joined the Navy and served for three years aboard the destroyer *Samuel B. Roberts*, which sailed out of Newport, Rhode Island. After getting discharged from the Navy, Mickey worked as a salesman at Schenectady Plymouth until a friend convinced him to apply to the Schenectady Police Force. He was hired and served for 23 years in many capacities, showing great aptitude for traffic-accident investigation and also as a member of the vice squad. Mickey was the president of the Policemen's Benevolent Association for some of this time. He then became a Determination Specialist for 12 years, working for a non-profit child welfare agency called Berkshire Farms, at which he interviewed youths who had broken the law, to determine the best way to help them get back on the right path. Mickey is now retired and lives with his wife, Alice, in Malta, New York. Mickey and Alice have two children, Michael and Melissa. Mickey still keeps in shape by visiting the gym every other day. He still looks like Tony Curtis.

JOHN BEZIO

John was on the *Union-Star* All-County team for two years in a row—quite an honor for the Goose-Hill-raised, rough-and-tumble young man who wanted more than anything to drive a truck like his father did. And that is what he did, starting in high school and continuing for the rest of his life. John drove his own truck for General Electric Company and any other firms that needed a reliable trucker. He was a member of the Teamsters, Local 294. He married his wife Lois in 1963, and they had two daughters, Dana and Rebecca. John died unexpectedly in 1979 from a heart attack. He was only 42 years old.

BOBBY PATRICK

Bobby was one of eight brothers that all played football at Mont Pleasant. He served in the U.S. Army for two years after graduating from Mont Pleasant. He then moved to Queens, New York, to work with his older brother, John (who had also played football at Mont Pleasant and was an All-County tackle in 1952) in the funeral home business. Bobby had only wanted to save up enough money to open a gas station back in Schenectady, but John persuaded him to go to funeral director school. Bob graduated from

American Academy McAllister Institute of Funeral Service in New York City and worked with John until 1965, when he moved to the western part of New York to purchase a funeral home. The deal fell through, and Bob moved to Clifter Springs, New York, where he purchased a funeral home and a furniture store. In 1972, John joined Bobby and they became partners in two funeral homes and furniture stores, one in Clifter Springs and the other in Phelps, New York. In 1980 they decided to go their separate ways. Bobby died in October of 2003 from emphysema. He and his wife Judith had three sons, Robert Jr., Michael, and Steven, and a daughter, Christine. Bob's son Michael continues to operate R.A. Patrick Corporation in Clifter Springs.

LARRY PIVACEK

During Larry's two years as the left end on the varsity team at Mont Pleasant, he had exactly three passes thrown to him. He caught all three and scored a touchdown each time, a perfect record. After graduating from high school, Larry had an opportunity to attend Cornell University on a football scholarship, but he decided instead to go to Potsdam State College to become a school music teacher. Larry graduated in 1959 and came back to Schenectady to teach at Oneida Middle School. In 1961, he married a Mont Pleasant girl, Margaret Clemante, and together they had five children: Larry, Christian, Andrew, Tristan, and Margaret, and 11 grandchildren. Larry continued his education at Union College, where in 1962, he received his Master of Education degree. Larry had a storied career in middle and elementary school music. He was an innovator in many music programs, including the All-Schools performance and his Senior Groups in which the students' parents performed. In 1966, Larry's high school football coach, at Mont Pleasant, Larry Mulvaney, recruited him to be his freshman coach, a position he held for 17 years. Larry fondly remembers all the help and advice he was given by another football coach at Mont Pleasant, Tony Parisi, who went on to become the principal at Mont Pleasant. Larry was a master carpenter and was in high demand in Schenectady for 35 years, doing repairs and remodeling. He purchased a 1909 four-story General Electric Plot home built on Rugby Road which had fallen into disrepair. He then completely gutted it and restored it to its former grandeur- a labor of love taking between two and three years to complete. Larry said it was his dream home, but as the taxes increased fourfold in 11 years, he decided it was time to sell. He moved to Rotterdam, New York, where he still lives with his wife, Margaret. Larry retired from teaching in 1992; and, outside of taking care of his own properties, also retired from his carpentry business.

JOE GREEN

Joe was probably the luckiest of all the 1954 All-County Football Team. He was only a junior in 1954, so he got to play Nott Terrace in 1955, when he was on the winning end, 21-0. So Joe got some closure that was denied to his fellow All-County teammates, since they were all seniors and had played their last high school football game. Joe never knew defeat on the football field during his high school playing years. Both his 1954 and his 1955 team went undefeated. After high school, Joe graduated from Schenectady Community College, and then worked for a division of General Electric for 33 years, where he became a supervisor. He was also active in the Mont Pleasant Booster Club and served as a committee member for the Schenectady City School District Athletic Hall of Fame. He was also, for 40 years, a proud member of the Schenectady Athletic Advisory Council. In his younger years, Joe was a member of the Jumping Jacks water ski team. He was married to his wife, Gail, for 43 years. He and Gail raised five nieces and nephews as their own. Joe died on February 5, 2014, in Schenectady.

MICKEY PETROLLE

After high school graduation, Al DeSantis, a *Union-Star* newspaper sportswriter, got Mickey a walk-on football tryout at Cornell University; but after about a month of bruising practices, 150-pound Mickey knew he just wasn't big enough, no matter how much he wanted to play college football or how hard he tried. So he left the team; and after one semester at Cornell, left college too. He returned to Schenectady and found employment at the GE in the drafting department, where he worked until 1957 when he joined the Army. After basic training, he married his high school sweetheart, Barbara Rolfe. He attended the Army's Fort Monmouth, New Jersey, Cryptograph Machine Repair School for one year. He was then stationed in Germany until his discharge in 1959.

In the 1960s, Mickey went to work for Manhattan Casualty Insurance Company as a salesman and branch manager. Mickey and Barbara divorced in the late 1960s. He then opened a partnership in a carpet company in Colonie, New York. He met his second wife Marie Houlihan Sherwood, a 1952 Mont Pleasant graduate; and in 1968, they had a daughter Julie. Marie contracted multiple sclerosis in 1969, and after four years could no longer work, requiring assistance in getting around. In 1979, Mickey and Marie decided to purchase a travel trailer, and they traversed the United States several times along with their daughter. They traveled for the next 14 years, always returning to the Schenectady area to visit relatives and friends. Mickey has worked for Knight Orchards in Burnt Hills since 1991, and at the age of 78 still picks apples every fall. Marie died in 1993. In 2001, after a hiatus of 54 years, Mickey decided to go back to college and started at S.U.N.Y. at Oneonta and graduated in 2009 with a B.S. in philosophy, a B.S. in psychology, and a minor in anthropology. Mickey now lives in Burnt Hills for six months of the year and St. Petersburg, Florida, for the other six months, staying in his travel trailer at both locations.

LOU DEMARCO

After graduation from Mont Pleasant, Lou served in the U.S. Army for two years. After learning the pizza business from his uncle John, who owned and operated Johnny DeMarco's Pizza on Michigan Avenue in Schenectady, Lou went on to own many pizza restaurants in Schenectady and was the founder of DeMarco's Restaurant on the Albany-Schenectady Road in Colonie. After moving to Florida, Lou opened DeMarco's Italian Restaurant on Madeira Beach. The restaurant was an instant success, enjoying a great reputation and a long run. Lou was a member of the American Legion in Madeira Beach. He was married three times and had a son, Louis Jr., and three daughters, Jacqueline, Toni, and Christine. Lou died in September of 2002.

RICHARD KACZMAREK

Richard received a full football scholarship to the American International College at Springfield, Massachusetts, but only played one semester before returning home to Schenectady. He married his wife, Jean, in 1959, and worked as a carpet salesman for John G. Myers Department Store in Albany, New York, for 18 years. When Myers closed, Richard went to work for Robinson's Furniture Company in Schenectady for many years. He is presently working at the Home Depot in Albany, New York, in the hardware department. Richard has two daughters and has been happily married to Jean for 53 years.

ED WILGOCKI

Upon graduation from high school, Ed joined the U.S. Army, where he was the driver of an anti-personnel carrier and was stationed in Germany for two years. When he came out of the Army, he became reacquainted with a young lady named Joan, who had lived right across the street from him since he was in the second grade. In 1959 Joan became his wife. Eddie worked for Tomac Builders for many years; and when that business closed, he opened his own general contracting firm. Ed was a master mason. He and his wife had two sons and were married for more than 40 years, living their entire lives in Schenectady. Ed died in March of 2003. Joan still lives in their family home in Mont Pleasant.

CHAPTER 18

Danny, Later

—————◆————

**"Few people I know have
played the hand as well as
Dan Monaco"
-John Cardillo**

AFTER GRADUATION, BRACES OR NOT, Danny knew he had to start thinking about the direction of his life. He had no money, no job, and no place of his own to lay his head; and he did not want to depend on anybody else for his needs. A friend who worked at Barney's Department Store on lower State Street in downtown Schenectady helped Danny get a job as a freight elevator operator. Danny knew he needed more than this to make a life for himself, so he took a civil service exam. He passed it and got an office job working for the State of New York in Albany.

While working there, he met co-worker Fran Vincaquerra, a Mont Pleasant girl whose family had moved to Rotterdam (a small town right next to Mont Pleasant), so she had attended Draper High School. She was a cheerleader at Draper in her early high school years, but when she turned 16, all she could think about was getting her driver's license, so she lost interest in cheerleading and dropped out. Fran and Danny didn't know each other in high school—besides attending different schools, she was two years younger than he. Fran was a cute, friendly, vivacious teenager who drove a flashy 1957 turquoise and white Chevrolet that her parents had given her for a high school graduation present. The '57 Chevy was one of the hottest cars of its day and is now one of the most sought-after collector cars. Fran and Danny fell in love, and in 1958 were married at Mount Carmel Catholic Church in the Hamilton Hill area. Their wedding reception was held at the popular Towne Tavern, right on the edge of Rotterdam and Mont Pleasant, and owned by Fran's Uncle Tony. There were over 500 people at the reception.

Still desiring to go further in life, Danny enrolled in evening classes at Russell Sage College, a former women's college in Troy, New York, that had recently opened a coed program in Albany. The governor of New York at the time, Nelson Rockefeller, endorsed a program in which the state offered a grant for full-time college students taking at least twelve credit hours, and Danny jumped at the opportunity.

The year 1959 brought their first child—a son, Jerry, named after Fran's father. After graduating from Russell Sage, Danny was planning to become a teacher. However, he and Fran discussed it and decided he should attend law school. He applied to the University of Miami, the University of Virginia, and the University of New Mexico, receiving acceptance to all three schools. By this time Fran's parents had moved to Naples, Florida, and encouraged the young family to relocate to Florida in order to be closer. So, Danny with his pick of three law schools, chose to attend the University of Miami to obtain his law degree. Back in October 1954, after receiving his devastating polio diagnosis, Danny could not have conjured up this scenario in his wildest dreams.

In 1964 Danny and Fran had another child, a girl this time; and they named her Laura. So with two babies in tow, they moved to Miami. They lived on campus in a dormitory that had been converted from an old boys' dorm into living space for families. Fran got a temporary job babysitting for a few months, and then found employment at the university in an office position. They had to leave the campus every summer when the school shut down for vacation, so they would drive back to Schenectady and stay with relatives for the summer. Over the summer, Fran worked two jobs—the night shift at General Electric and as a secretary for the Schenectady District Attorney. Danny clerked for the well-known lawyer Nick Morsilla for $25 a week, and between them they were able to save up enough money to cover their living expenses in Miami for the next school year. This was their life for three years until Danny graduated in 1969. Both Danny and Fran worked hard, having nothing handed to them. Danny not only worked hard but hit the books hard too.

After graduation they returned to Schenectady, where Danny joined Nick Morsilla's Law Firm; however, the dangers of the icy winter roads and sidewalks made it difficult for him to get around. So he packed up his family again and headed to sunny Naples, Florida, where he worked with Attorney Walter Sorokoty. Danny later became a founding partner with the law firm of Monaco, Cardillo, and Keith. One of Danny's former law partners, John Cardillo, recalled Danny saying, *"You play the hand you're dealt with."* In his speech at a 2008 ceremony honoring Monaco with a Lifetime Achievement Award from the National Italian-American Bar Association, Cardillo said, "Few people I know have played the hand as well as Dan Monaco."

In 1996 Danny left his law firm to seek a circuit court judgeship in Collier County, Florida. Danny won the election against a Fort Myers lawyer. He had again turned the page on a new chapter in his life.

In the same 2008 speech, Cardillo went on to list Danny's many accomplishments as a judge and lawyer:

He served as president of Collier County Bar Association and was a member of the Roscoe Pound Foundation, a "sociological jurisprudence" group named after a former Harvard Law School dean and author. He was certified in civil trial practice and was Naples' first certified marital and family law attorney. He was commissioner and chair of the 20th Circuit Judicial Nominating Commission, and founder and chairman of its Family Law Section. He was also Chair of the Family Law Section of the Academy of Florida Trial Lawyers, and a sustaining member of the American Trial Lawyers and its Family Law Section.

In the opportunity of a lifetime, Danny attended Oxford University in England. Oxford University is pretty heady stuff for a poor boy from Schenectady, New York.

Cardillo told the group that Danny had "distinguished himself on the bench, as he had in private practice, with the same quality of work, integrity, perseverance, and charm."

About 120 people—attorneys, judges, friends, and his second wife Ann —attended the ceremony honoring Monaco for his life-time achievement award. Collier County Bar Association President, Kathleen Passidomo, said many others wanted to attend but they had to be turned away due to lack of space. Danny, who hit the mandatory retirement age of seventy, was forced to retire at the end of 2008.

CHAPTER 19

Sonny, Later

Sonny DeVito, age 22

"I know one thing though-it would've been a great game"
-Sonny DeVito

AFTER GRADUATING FROM HIGH SCHOOL, Sonny attended Siena College in Albany, New York, for one semester, and then finished his degree at Spencer Business College in Schenectady.

Sonny then found employment with the City of Schenectady working as a dispatcher for the Bureau of Public Services. He always loved cars, so he got involved with stock car racing as an owner. He couldn't drive race cars, but he could do just about anything else with the car, including building it and keeping it in repair. His first racecar was a 1955 Chevy Sportsman #39, which raced at Fonda Speedway. Ex-teammate Al Burnham also raced and was sometimes in competition with Sonny's cars. Sonny married Dorothy Finley in 1965 and they had two children together, Oliver Jr. (nicknamed Skipper) in 1970 and Diane in 1971. After becoming friends with Bea Schmitt in 1972, they became romantically involved four years later, which led to their marriage in 1982.

In 1981 Sonny's son wanted to play football, so Sonny decided to get involved with Skipper's Pop Warner football team in Rotterdam. Sonny was asked to be the defensive coach and held that post for the next three seasons. In his fourth year of coaching, he was asked to be the head coach, and he accepted the position. Rotterdam lost its first two games under Sonny, but then got rolling and won the next five. Sonny also coached Rotterdam Babe Ruth Baseball but just couldn't get interested in baseball like he was interested in his first love—football. Sonny coached Pop Warner until 1993.

After 35 years of service, Sonny retired from the city in 1992. He had attained the position of automotive stock clerk and office manager. When Sonny was 46 years old he was asked who he thought would have won that 1954 Election Day matchup. He grinned and said, "Hey, you're not going to get me to answer that. That's something that they've been talking about for 30 years. I still don't know who would have won. I know one thing though—it would have been a great game."

Danny Smith, a younger co-worker, helped Sonny build one of his racecars and remembered one day working on one side of the car while Sonny was doing some cutting with a torch on the car's other side. Suddenly Sonny started yelling, and then propelled his wheelchair so quickly toward an outside water faucet that he couldn't stop, ending up crashing into the house. A piece of hot slag had broken off and fallen into his boot. Talk about a hot boot! Danny also remembers that Sonny was quiet and never talked about polio or the consequences it had in his life. Danny first met *Ollie** when he was 16 years old and had just been hired to work at the city garage where Ollie also worked. Danny thought that Ollie was the coolest person he had ever met, as Ollie had just purchased a red automatic 1965 Chevelle with red interior and mag wheels. It was specially fitted with hand controls so Ollie could drive it. Danny's passion was also cars, so he idolized Ollie. Danny raced with Ollie at Malta Speedway, Fonda Speedway, Victoria Speedway, and any other track they could get to and race on.

After contracting polio Sonny lived his entire life in a wheelchair, but that didn't slow him down in anything he desired to do, whether it was working, coaching football, building racecars, cooking, driving, or raising his children. One of the things Sonny enjoyed (that didn't matter whether or not he was in a wheelchair) was playing poker. He played on a regular basis with his uncle, cousins, and anybody else willing to take him on in a very competitive 5-, 10-, or 25-cent game.

After the kids had all grown up and moved out of the house and when money was not so tight, Ollie and Bea started to vacation at York Beach in Maine. Ollie's grandfather had once owned an old-fashioned four-story wooden hotel right on Short Sands Beach. His grandfather started with five cottages on a nearby beach called Wells Beach, then after a few years sold the cottages and bought the hotel. Ollie and Bea had been able to stay at the hotel one year out of the six or seven years they visited York Beach. Ollie enjoyed sitting up on the cliffs overlooking the beach and watching Bea walk the shoreline.

---

* Both Danny and Sonny's wife, Bea, called Sonny, Ollie, along with many others.

Sonny and Bea were both deeply involved with the Rotterdam Elks Club and its Youth Sports Program. Bea was the treasurer and Sonny was on the cooking team, manning the fryers and cooking burgers and hot dogs. They were active until Sonny's health problems started to get the best of him. In 2000 Sonny had a quintuple heart bypass; and after that he joined a group called Warriors on Wheels, which met twice a week at a local gym. For the next three years, Sonny worked on rebuilding his upper body strength, which he had lost due to his heart problems. In 2004 Sonny needed surgery on his toes, which had become gangrenous and needed to be amputated. He suffered a heart attack while on the operating table and died a few weeks later.

Sonny's children and his stepchildren all remember him as a terrific father who was always there for them, no matter what.

CHAPTER 20

Athletic Hall of Fame and Reunion Dinner

—◆—

"Without Walt Przybylo there is no Pat Riley"
-Pat Riley

SCHENECTADY WAS A SPORTS TOWN gone wild in the early- and mid-1950s. The city had a minor league Class A baseball team called the Schenectady Blue Jays that played at McNearney Stadium. The Blue Jays were affiliated with the Philadelphia Phillies, and in the 1953 season went 86-65. Not many towns this size had their own professional baseball team. Schenectady Little Leaguers went all the way to the championship game in 1953, but lost out to Birmingham, Alabama, in a pitching contest which ended 1-0. Manager Mike Maietta, in a seeming losers' tirade, promised the spectators, the officials, and the city of Williamsport, Pennsylvania, that they would be back the next year and win it all. And guess what? They did. Schenectady born and bred Lee Wallard won the Indianapolis 500 in 1951, leading the race 159 laps out of 200 and becoming the first driver to finish the full 500 miles in under four hours. Tony Parisi, a 1951 Mont Pleasant High School graduate, was named an All New England football player at Holy Cross in 1953.

So many great athletes came out of the Schenectady school system that it would take another chapter or two to list all of the great baseball players, basketball players, football players, boxers, bowlers...and the list goes on and on. So in 1997 when the superintendent, Dr. Ray Colucciello, suggested that Schenectady city schools needed its own Hall of Fame, nobody thought it was a crazy idea. Furthermore, it was natural that of the first eleven inductees, nine of them were from the 1950s era of sports in Schenectady.

The original Schenectady High School was opened in 1903 to serve grades 10, 11 and 12. It was the only high school in Schenectady. In 1931 the school's name was changed to Nott Terrace when Mont Pleasant High School opened as Schenectady's second high school. By 1958, Nott Terrace was overcrowded with 1,500 students: both the boys' and girls' gyms were cramped, its library could only accommodate 80 students, and the cafeteria only held 250 students. There were also problems with fire escapes, plumbing, and stairwells. The building had not aged well, so the school district decided to build a replacement school on The Plaza in the much nicer neighborhood of Union Street, about one-and-a-half miles away from Nott Terrace. It was named Linton High School after Dr. Harry T. Linton, who had been the superintendent of Schenectady schools in 1946. Then in 1992 Linton High School and Mont Pleasant High School were consolidated, and the only remaining high school in Schenectady was once again called Schenectady High School. Talk about coming full circle.

In 1997 Schenectady High School wanted to rename their indoor athletic facility the Pat Riley Sports Center. Pat was a 1963 graduate of Linton High School who went on to play basketball at the University of Kentucky for the legendary coach Adolph Rupp, then was a first round draft choice (7th overall pick) of the San Diego Rockets in 1967. He joined the Los Angeles Lakers in 1970. Once his playing years were over, he became head coach of the team in 1981. Schenectady High School wanted to honor one of its favorite sons by renaming the gymnasium after him, but Riley humbly declined. Pat thought that his former coach at Linton, Walt Przybylo, who had won seven league championships, had a 46-game winning streak, and coached two undefeated teams, rightfully deserved the honor. As Pat said, "Without Walt Przybylo, there is no Pat Riley."

The superintendent of schools, Dr. Ray Colucciello, got Riley to change his mind with a promise that the Schenectady City School District was about to start a Hall of Fame and that Coach Przybylo would surely be one of its first inductees. At the initial brainstorming meeting with others interested in Schenectady School District sports, Dr. Colucciello came up with the idea to open the nominations to anyone who had either coached or played sports at a Schenectady school. Bob Pezzano, a special education teacher at Schenectady High School, was named chairman by Dr. Colucciello, and there you had the birth of the Schenectady City School District Athletic Hall of Fame and Reunion Dinner. Bob approached Tony Cristello, a 1961 Mont Pleasant graduate and local artist, asking him if he would come up with an idea for individual plaques to commemorate each inductee. Cristello replied, "Give me about a week." At the next meeting, he returned with the concept of a bronze plaque fashioned after the three-dimensional bas-reliefs of the inductees in the Baseball Hall of Fame at Cooperstown, New York.

In 1998, the first five inductees were all coaches. First, was Bill Eddy, a Harvard graduate who began his coaching career at the first Schenectady High School in 1920. He coached basketball, speed-skating, cross-country, and track. Bill coached cross-country for 26 years and won 17 national championship titles. In the 1940s he went on to coach cross-country at Rensselaer Polytechnic Institute in Troy, New York, and then became Director of Parks and Recreation in Schenectady for about 20 years.

Second was the legendary Sig Makofski. Sig, a former sports star at Schenectady High School, graduated from Union College and went on to play professional basketball. Sig started his coaching career at his alma mater in 1926. When Mont Pleasant opened in 1931, he became its first basketball coach and remained the coach until 1952, when he became head of physical education and director of athletics well into the 1960s. His unbelievable record of 354-24 included six undefeated seasons and winning streaks of 46, 42, 39, and 36 games. At one reunion dinner an attendee, who had been looking at Sig's plaque inscribed with the 354-24 record, mentioned to Bob Pezzano that they must have left a number off the *24*. Bob said, "No, that's the record." Sig also coached football and had gone four seasons undefeated. His combined Schenectady High School and Mont Pleasant High School football and basketball record was 461-35, a winning percentage of 92.9%. Unbelievable. Many sports enthusiasts in Schenectady point to Sig Makofski as the foundation for the rich history of sports in the city. Sig also won two New York State Golf Championships and was honored at the Basketball Hall of Fame in Springfield, Massachusetts, in 1981.

Next up, Coach Larry Mulvaney. Larry came to Mont Pleasant in 1952, where he coached wrestling, football, and track. His football record at Mont Pleasant was an impressive 101-67-7 He coached three undefeated football teams and had the number one team in New York State in 1967, chosen by sportswriters from the entire state.

The fourth inductee, as promised, was Walt Przybylo. He was a graduate of Mont Pleasant and Cortland College, and in 1952 began teaching and coaching boys' basketball, baseball, football, and golf at Nott Terrace. When Linton High School opened in 1958, Walt was named head basketball coach. His first love was basketball, and he held a record of 270-96 (Nott Terrace and Linton combined). He had two undefeated teams at Linton, seven league championships, and at one time a 46-game winning streak. He coached Barry Kramer and Pat Riley, both of whom went on to become NBA players.

The fifth was Ray Vacca, a 1935 graduate of Nott Terrace. Ray started his teaching career at Nott Terrace in 1945 and two years later switched over to Mont Pleasant. In the early 1950s, Coach Vacca started coaching track and field and cross-country. Over a

20 year period, Coach Vacca's track and field teams won 16 sectional dual-meet championships. When Sig Makofski was named Athletic Director in 1952, Vacca took over the basketball team and had a successful record.

There you have the first five inductees into the Schenectady City School District Athletic Hall of Fame. It was certainly going to be a tough bunch to follow for future nominees.

The first reunion dinner was held at Glen Sanders Mansion in Scotia, New York. The historic mansion was built in the 1700s along the banks of the picturesque Mohawk River and was now a restaurant, banquet hall, and hotel. It is owned by Angelo Mazzone. Angelo so impressed the Hall of Fame organization that he would go on to cater every annual reunion dinner, even though in its third year the venue was changed to the Hall of Springs in Saratoga Springs due to space requirements. Angelo Mazzone had been a supporter of the Hall of Fame since its inception. There were numerous comments about the reunion dinner not being held in Schenectady, the board of directors at the Hall of Fame did not feel Schenectady had an adequate venue; so the dinner stayed at Saratoga until 2008, when it moved to the Proctor's Theatre on State Street in downtown Schenectady.

Proctor's Theatre (which officially stylized its name to *Proctors* in 2007) is a former vaudeville house built in 1926 in the heyday of vaudeville. It cost 1.5 million dollars (20 million in modern dollars) to build, and opened on December 27, 1926, with a showing of the silent film *Stranded in Paris*. The audience was so impressed by the lavish facilities that no one complained about the malfunctioning Wurlitzer organ. The theatre had fallen into disrepair throughout the 1960s and 1970s, and it was slated to be torn down to become a parking lot until a group of activists joined together and created the Arts District of Schenectady and saved Proctors Theatre from the wrecking ball.

In the fall of 2007, Proctors finished a 24.5 million dollar expansion, and Schenectady had a state-of-the-art facility. At their annual meeting in Cleveland, in 2009, the theatre won the Outstanding Historic Theatre Award presented by the League of Historic American Theatres.

Chairman Bob Pezzano wasn't exactly sure how the *rest* of the committee felt, but as far as *he* was concerned Angelo Mazzone had to be on the list of Proctors approved caterers, or else it was a dead deal. Proctors quickly gave the approval, and the Hall of Fame found a new home for its annual reunion dinner. Bob Iovinella, owner of Hollywood Visual Productions in Schenectady, greatly appreciated the state-of-the-art audio and video equipment that was available to him at Proctors. Bob, whose son was the wrestling coach at Linton in 1998, had done the sound and visual production since the start of the Hall of Fame.

Over the years, various schools and organizations have contacted Bob Pezzano asking for advice on starting their own Hall of Fame. Bob has been as helpful as he could be in order to start them off on the right track, but in the back of his mind he was always thinking, "They may have the athletes, but where are they going to find a Tony Cristello or Bob Iovinella?" The Schenectady Hall of Fame has been blessed to have men and women of Tony's and Bob's caliber to set Schenectady's Hall of Fame apart as the granddaddy of them all.

CHAPTER 21

Legacy Tribute

—————

**"You're a champion until
someone beats you."
-Sig Makofski**

DANNY MONACO HAD NEVER "FELT that sick before, or since" that
Saturday practice just prior to the classic Mont Pleasant-Nott
Terrace Election Day game. Yet as bad as he felt he knew "there
was no way in hell he was going to miss that game." That was the
sentiment among all the players, coaches, and fans. After being
first postponed, and then canceled altogether due to the risk of
infection by the polio virus, the feeling of disappointment was
overshadowed by the tremendous concern for Danny and Sonny,
and the fearfulness that others could possibly contract it as well.
Each team also had one additional game on their 1954 schedules
which was canceled. Even though both teams were powerhouses
that had soundly trounced all of the other teams in their Class A
league, neither could be named champion because of a district
rule that stated in order to win the championship, *all* of the team's
scheduled games had to be played.

Technically, Troy High and Amsterdam High, that had played
at Amsterdam Field on the Saturday after Election Day, were
the only ones eligible. Neither team had won a league game all
year. Mont Pleasant and Nott Terrace had each beaten Troy and

Amsterdam by a combined score of 200-20. So much for bragging rights for the 1954 Class A Champions.

A story in the Schenectady *Union-Star* regarding the 1954 Mont Pleasant/Nott Terrace game proclaimed: "Powerful, rugged, well coached, the undefeated teams should wage a battle worthy of discussion for years." The article turned out to be prophetic, but for an entirely different reason.

Players on both teams are still haunted by the mystery of the unknown outcome of this game. At a reunion of players from both teams, Mickey Petrolle, a Mont Pleasant star who played both offense and defense, said, "Let's settle this right now; let's put on the pads and go out to the parking lot right now. Forget the pads—let's go!" Even though the former players were in their 70s with all the aches and pains that accompany that age, they all seemed ready to go. But that wasn't going to happen. What *was* going to happen was a legacy tribute to these teams whose rivalry symbolized the spirit of high school sports, to be held at the district's Athletic Hall of Fame ceremonies and reunion dinner on September 14, 2009.

During interviews prior to the legacy tribute, Al Burnham, a Nott Terrace star who was named 1954 All-County halfback, remembered, "A couple of days prior it was called off, and it was like pulling the rug out from under you." Danny Monaco also recalled, "The big thing was both teams were undefeated. The game had built to a crescendo. Everybody I knew in Schenectady was going to go to it; and as I understand, the bookmakers were getting a lot of action. The odds went both ways. Just all around, it was building into a great game. We remembered the teams playing each other since we were kids, and that built it up for us."

The idea for the legacy tribute was initially suggested by Bruce Vacca, a 1968 Linton High School graduate who was a police officer in Schenectady, New York. According to Bob Pezzano, the chairman of the Schenectady City School District Athletic Hall of Fame, the concept had already been considered by the Hall of

Fame committee, so Bruce's suggestion was further confirmation that it was time to make it happen.

About a week prior to the tribute, the captains of the respective teams got together to shoot some footage for a video that was to be shown at the event. Danny Monaco represented Mont Pleasant, and Alonzo Burnham and Nick Ronca represented Nott Terrace. Danny and Alonzo had never actually met until that day. After the three men reminisced, Burnham said, "I'll tell you, it was good to see them. Our season wasn't finished yet; then when that came up they told us, 'Turn in your equipment.' It was a hard thing to do, how it ended. We were saying, 'Geez, isn't there something else we can do, like play a football game or something? Can we wrestle them?' But there was nothing to be done. The season's done. That's it."

"I don't know what to say—it's great for everybody," Monaco said. "I'm in awe of the fact that they're honoring both teams. It's deserved and it brought back a lot of memories. All of us were full of bravado, but that was a tough team. In my opinion it would've been a tossup.

Probably the best thing that happened out of the tragedy of polio was nobody came out a loser and both ended up winners. I saw (former teammate) Mike Ferraro a few days ago, and he said, Maybe this will bring closure. I'm not sure if that's a fact."

Mike Petrolle of Mont Pleasant and Nick Ronca of Nott Terrace were each positive that their own team would have won. No *ifs*, *ands*, or *buts*.

On September 14, 2009, Proctors hosted the 12th Annual Schenectady City School District Athletic Hall of Fame and Reunion Dinner. Pat Riley, the five-time NBA Championship head coach and 2008 Naismith Basketball Hall of Fame inductee from Linton High was the guest speaker. The two Hall of Fame inductees in 2009 were Dick Bennett (known as Dick Bednarkiewicz during high school), one of legendary Head Coach Sig Makofski's greatest players, who had played varsity basketball at Mont Pleasant from 1937 to 1940; and Mike Meola, who had played three years of varsity football, basketball, and baseball at Linton High, and was a first team All-County selection in all three sports during his junior and senior years, Schenectady's first athlete to achieve this honor. Both Dick and Mike spoke before the two teams were introduced.

Also receiving recognition with a legacy tribute were the undefeated 1954 football team players from Mont Pleasant and Nott Terrace, who had been only a few days away from the classic Election Day football game when players Danny Monaco from Mont Pleasant and Sonny DeVito from Nott Terrace were both stricken with polio. The game had been canceled, leaving everyone, players and fans alike, wondering what the outcome might have been.

Craig Brown has been the Master of Ceremonies since the start of the Hall of Fame in 1998. Craig graduated from Mont Pleasant High School in 1963, and from 1994 to 2002 was the principal of Schenectady High School. He had the honor of introducing keynote speaker Pat Riley to the over 600 guests who had just dined on an excellent dinner catered by Mazzone Hospitality.

Pat Riley, a 2000 inductee into the Hall of Fame and a 1963 Linton graduate, knew most of the people at the dinner, so he didn't really need much of an introduction. Pat came to the podium with his immaculately-groomed and impeccably-dressed trademark look—hair slicked back, wearing an expensive dark blue Armani suit. Whether the suit makes the man or the man makes the suit, either way, Pat looked like an advertisement out of *GQ* magazine. One of the first things Pat spoke about was the 1962 Mont Pleasant-Linton Election Day football game in which he was Linton's quarterback. You can be worth 80 million dollars, possess five NBA Championship rings, and have had a brilliant career in sports—or maybe you were just a third- string scrub who rarely got to play in a game—but everybody who played in the Mont Pleasant –Nott Terrace / Linton Election Day game in Schenectady remembered the outcome of the game. The score, the plays, the game-day weather...everything. Nobody had to remind Pat Riley, an All-American Quarterback that year, about his senior year at Linton playing against Mont Pleasant—he remembered it vividly. He said he was sorry the 1954 players didn't get to play their game, and that only someone who *did play*, and *lost*, could understand. That got quite a laugh. Pat's, up until then undefeated, Linton football team lost 14-13 in the final seconds of the game.

Next, Pat credited one of the inductees of the Hall of Fame that night, fellow teammate Mike Meola, as the person who helped him turn his life from being a juvenile delinquent to a serious student and dedicated athlete. Pat talked about how his parents, his friends' parents, his teachers, and his coaches had a huge impact on his life, and how without them his almost unbelievable career in basketball would not have been possible. Pat is a much sought-after motivational speaker who commands fees of $50,000 plus for his ability to tailor his message to his listeners. He did not disappoint anyone that night. A source that asked to remain anonymous verified that Pat has never charged the Schenectady Hall of Fame a penny for all the work he has done for them over the years. Pat Riley is truly one of Schenectady's gems.

Next up was Dick Bennett, a 1940 Mont Pleasant High School graduate who was one of the two inductees that night. Dick walked with a cane, probably due to a lifetime of pounding the boards in basketball. With a mind as sharp as a tack and a clear, loud voice, Dick thanked the Hall of Fame, saying he shared the honor with all of his teammates without whom he would not have been there that night.

Mike Meola, the other inductee of the night and a 1963 graduate of Linton High School, spoke next. Mike, who had played sports and graduated with Pat Riley, credited his parents, his grandfather, endless days of sandlot sports, and his coaches for his athletic success. Mike was a Schenectady School District teacher and coach for 38 years, and the first athlete in Schenectady to receive a first team All-County Selection in all three sports that he played- football, basketball, and baseball.

After Mike's acceptance speech, Craig Brown called all of the 1954 football players to be seated up on the stage and introduced them one at a time to the audience. He first introduced the 16 Mont Pleasant players in attendance and asked them to stand when he called their names. Jim Poirier (one of the only two freshman on the 1954 varsity team), Vince Savini, Peter von Rogov, Dick Koretnicki (the other freshman), Nick Colamarino, John Di Cocco, Vince Riggi, Vinny Vardine, Danny Greco, Vince Gallo, Carmen DiVietro, Larry Pivacek, Joe Green, Mickey Petrolle, Mickey Ferraro, and Danny Monaco. Emcee Craig Brown then mentioned two players on the Nott Terrace team who could not make the presentation because of conflicts and said, "I don't know what could be more important," which got a nervous laugh from the crowd. Then the Nott Terrace players were called: Mike Delvin, Don Schermerhorn, Tony Mauro, Nick Ronca, Dick Kaczmarek (who had left early), Al Burnham, Derry Cooke, Assistant Coach Chuck Abba, and Junior Varsity Assistant Coach Roy Larson. Next Craig called Tommy Brennan, a 2001 Hall of Fame inductee, up to the stage to officiate at the coin toss. Tommy was a 1938 Mont Pleasant graduate who had refereed over 4,100 games in his career. Representing Mont Pleasant at the coin toss was Co-captain Danny Monaco, and representing Nott Terrace were Derry Cooke, Al Burnham, and Nick Ronca. Tommy said that Terrace should make the call since they were the older school. Derry Cooke called tails, and tails it was; so Chuck Abba stepped up to the podium to speak for Nott Terrace.

CHUCK ABBA'S SPEECH

I thought if we lost the toss, they could refer to my age and say it's okay to go ahead.

Bob Pezzano asked me to say a few words and said please limit it to about six or seven minutes. What Bob didn't realize at the time is that whenever you ask a teacher to limit something to six or seven minutes, you're asking for trouble. I'm very honored to represent the coaches of the Nott Terrace High School 1954 undefeated team. But the true honor this evening really belongs to the man who is no longer with us, Mr. Pete Shulha. Pete, in my estimation, was a dedicated, hardworking, and excellent teacher. As Craig pointed out earlier, he went 12 straight games with these two teams and his assistant was, of course, Mr. Roy Larson, who coached the JV team. But as Pat Riley was talking this evening, I was thinking about the qualities that he talked about in a coach or a teacher. In my estimation, Pete Shulha had those qualities. He was a good coach, he was a good teacher, and he was a good friend to all of his players. He was concerned about them at all times, and he was a good role model for them; and so on behalf of him, I'm honored to be here this evening.

I was part of the history, if you will, of the decision to postpone the game. My recollection, remember, is 55 years ago, so bear with me if I miss anything. Mr. Abbey, the principal (Roy Abbey, the principal of Nott Terrace High School) called us into his office—I believe it was a Monday morning—and informed us, as we had already known, that Oliver DeVito and Danny Monaco from Mont Pleasant were in the hospital with polio. He told us that Dr. Gomer Richards, whose sons Gomer and Dick Richards played at the Nott Terrace games, would be up shortly to discuss the situation with us. Subsequently, Pete and I went down to the spacious, beautiful Nott Terrace gym office, which reeked of athleticism from about 50 years, and we waited, patiently, of course. Dr. Richards came into the office, and he said, "I'm sorry to tell you gentlemen, but the game has to be postponed." He had met with the county and city health officers, he had met with a group of doctors, and the feeling among all of them was if we played the game and other players came down with polio, we'd never be able to live with ourselves. I can picture

Pete Shulha to this day—when Pete was upset with something his jaws would work, you could see those muscles cringing—but he accepted it quickly. We all did—I mean we really had no choice.

So that day and since then the speculation has begun; and incidentally, the town getting ready for Election Day was as disappointed as we were. And so, that speculation began in 1954 about who was the better team and who would've won, and you know what? It's a very difficult thing to call. And I'll tell you what, Election Day was probably the most electrifying and most meaningful game that any players and any team could possibly play. It meant everything to them. I know what I'm saying because I played in the 1942 and 1943 Election Day games at Mont Pleasant. So I know both sides of the coin. I knew how these kids felt, both from Mont Pleasant and Nott Terrace. They were broken-hearted and disappointed. But to try to say which team would win is, to me—I would say even to this day—is extremely difficult. Because, as I said, both teams had great athletes. So I went back to an old adage that I learned from a great coach, Sig Makofski- you're the champion until somebody beats you. You're the champion until somebody beats you. Sitting on the stage this evening are a group of men from both high schools that have never been beaten. Consequently, in my opinion, they are co-champions and can be proud of that for the rest of their lives.

Danny was helped to the podium by Al Burnham, Derry Cooke, and Nick Ronca, who protectively circled him and remained standing during his entire speech. While Danny was co- captain of the Mont Pleasant football team, his defensemen were, naturally, all Mont Pleasant boys; but tonight he would be surrounded by the guys from Nott Terrace. There was a stool behind Danny for him to use if necessary, but he first stood and braced himself by holding onto the sides of the podium. He struggled a bit, and after a while Al helped Danny sit back on the stool, which seemed to help him to become more relaxed and steady. During the speech, Al

Burnham wiped away a few tears, and after Danny finished speaking Al hugged him and helped him back to his seat.

Danny's Speech

I'm going to speak up, only because I've been talking to my class-mates and I've noticed that every other word I get back is "Huh?" On behalf of Derry Cooke, and Al Burnham, and Nick Ronca, and members of both teams, we would like to thank the Hall of Fame committee that organized this event; and I especially would like to thank Bob Pezzano, who accommodated me on every request I had and answered every question I had. I would also like to mention the fact that Mike Meola and Dick Bennett really deserved their awards as inductees, and I would like to congratulate them. Firstly, I grew up with a lot of people from Polish descent; I'm glad Dick Bennett changed his name—that would have had me stumped. We would also like to congratulate Craig Brown for doing such a great job as emcee and Pat Riley for his inspiring keynote speech. I also would like to thank Al, Derry, and Nick for allowing me to speak on behalf of both teams.

Now, if anybody here thinks I'm going to say anything derogatory about the Nott Terrace team with these three guys around me, you're a little foggy. You know Nick and Derry gave a one-two punch that was great for a quarter- and fullback, and Derry's record speaks for itself, but I really think that my friend Vince Gallo and I weren't too bad either. What do you think? When I spoke with Nick, I thought he was a really intelligent fellow and married a girl from our '55 class...

You know, I think I would be remiss if I didn't mention two people who are not here tonight. One is Ollie DeVito. Ollie lay in the bed across from me for about four months, and Ollie had true grit. He came into the hospital around Christmas time, and because it was so full we were put in isolation together. I don't know what that meant; apparently we couldn't give to each other what we had. But in any case, Ollie decided that he was going to sing Christmas carols. We got the whole ward going that was in isolation, and the nurses were so thankful to Ollie for starting. Ollie had the voice I didn't, and Ollie was a funny guy too; he had a great sense of humor. True story: I heard at 2 o'clock in the morning one time, 'Danny, there's a mouse on the floor between our beds.' I said to Ollie, 'Well, get rid of it.' So he took his urinal and threw it at it. True story. That mouse never came back. Naturally, Ollie was very uncomfortable all night.

You know, Ollie loved cars, he loved to hunt, and he loved to go to spring training camp for the New York Giants. And nothing stopped him despite the fact he was in a wheelchair. He was a great guy, and I'm glad his wife and his son are here tonight. The other person I wish was here is my friend, Lou DeMarco. Lou and I were friends from kindergarten on, and I remember him calling me when I was elected co-captain. I hadn't been at school that day. And he said, 'Danny, we were elected co-captains. It would really mean something if we went undefeated.' And I said, 'Gee, I can't believe Lou thinks we're gonna do that. But Lou, you got your wish, we're undefeated.'

Bob Pezzano said, 'Danny, don't speak any more than eight minutes to ten minutes.' And it's hard to summarize what the feelings are of all these great guys in that short period of time. But I'm just going to give you a few snippets of what some of them have said to me, and I think it represents how all of them feel. When I saw Al Burnham at a videotaping, we both, I think, became a little emotional. And Al said one word: 'Memories.' And you know, that should be the theme of my talk today because there are a lot of memories that were brought back. Nick said, 'It would've been a tough game.' I think that was an understatement. I think it would've been a really tough game. My friend Mike Petrolle said, 'You know, Dan, we play for each other and we didn't want to let each other down.' That was important. And my friend Mike Ferraro said,

'You know, I hope this brings closure for both teams,' and I hope it does too.

You know, we were the first class that Coach Larry Mulvaney had for three years, and he can't be here tonight due to illness. But I recall going into the tenth grade and someone saying to me, 'We got a new coach and he's from a foreign country—Chicopee, Massachusetts.' Well, you know, looking back at his record he didn't do too, too bad for an immigrant. I'd like you to indulge me just a few minutes so I can relay to you my feelings about that year and that team.

You know, the Nott Terrace-Mont Pleasant game was a dream for all of us that grew up and wanted to play football. It was the ultimate. And as the season progressed and as we all, both teams, were undefeated, it became the dream of all three classes in each high school; and then it became the dream of the city. I think the whole Schenectady population was involved in that game. McNearney Stadium was sold out early. I don't think anybody was going to vote that day very frankly.

That dream came to an end for me on a rainy, cold Saturday about 55 years ago. I woke up that morning, and I felt more pain than I ever had; and I was running a fever that wouldn't stop. But there was no way in hell I was going to miss that game. So, I went to practice, and I think some of my classmates saw that I wasn't doing that well. As a matter of fact, I remember one incident where I was supposed to be Derry Cooke and I broke to the right. I don't know how that happened—I think these guys were sleeping, they weren't paying attention. Tony Parisi said, 'Boy, you guys can't stop the first-string fullback, can you?' And I said, Tony, don't say that. I feel bad enough as it is; they're going to kill me out there. But, in any case, as I said, the dream came to an end for me on that day. Coach Mulvaney sent me home, said go shower, get ready to come back on television (which was a tradition at that time—the co-captains and coaches appeared on television and were interviewed), and take care of yourself. Well, I never made that television interview. Never made it to the game, but nobody else did either.

I recall something that great sportswriter Grantland Rice wrote, and he said something like this, 'When the Great Scorer in the sky comes to mark against your game, he'll mark not if you won or lost, but how you played the game.' When he comes to mark against our teams, both of them, I'm sure he'll mark that we played the game with a tough desire to win, an abiding loyalty to each other, and a lot of pride. I want to thank all of you for coming tonight, I want to thank both members of our teams. Thank you.

That's it, that's the story. It ends right there. Remember, this is a true story. In the Prologue I said I was going to tell the story as it actually happened. I did. Sometimes true stories don't have a real happy ending...just an ending.

—————◆—————

HALLOWED GROUND

Are they still there?

THIS IS THE POINT IN most books where the author tells you what happened later in the lives of the principals in the story, but that information has been shared throughout the book, so you already know how their lives turned out. Instead, this book will take a different approach.

Growing up in Schenectady, there were certain places that the locals considered *hallowed ground*. You know, places you hope will never change, even a little bit: schools, hangouts, swimming holes. What happened to the ones mentioned in this book? Are they still there? Are they still the same? Let's start with the big picture and work down. So first: What happened to Schenectady?

WHAT EVER HAPPENED TO SCHENECTADY?

**As General Electric
goes, so goes the
city.**

In 1954 Schenectady's population was 92,000 with 35,000 people
working at GE and 15,000 employed at ALCO. The downtown had
three large department stores, five movie theaters, three five- and
ten-cent stores, restaurants and bars galore, and a host of other
supporting stores and businesses. Along with these, the entire city
was flourishing; there never seemed to be an empty storefront. In
the neighborhoods, everyone left their doors unlocked and everyone knew their neighbors. If you needed a little credit at the corner store until payday, you got it – no questions asked. Gas station
attendants pumped your gas. They also checked your water and
oil, and washed your windshield, all with a smile on their faces. No
charge. It was a golden era for Schenectady...for many other places
in America as well, but Schenectady for sure.

The problem started small; but like a snowball rolling down a
hill, it picked up in both speed and form as it went along. First,
in 1956 GE became dissatisfied with its partnership manufacturing
locomotives with ALCO and started building domestic road locomotives itself. ALCO gradually gave way to the competition from GE and
in 1969 closed its Schenectady plant, selling its designs to the Montreal
Locomotive Works in Canada. Bye-bye, U.S. jobs. Additionally, in
the late 50's and early 60's, the big competitive unions at GE, IUE,
and UE were constantly either threatening strikes or calling strikes
for higher wages and better benefits. GE warned them over and over
that things were different now, and that worldwide competition was
forcing GE to either get much more competitive with its own pricing
or else lose out on bids to other companies. They said they could not
afford the strikes or the demands the unions were making.

Nevertheless, the unions pushed back, forcing GE to relocate thousands of manufacturing jobs to the Sun Belt, where there was no union representation. Instead there was a "right-to-work" law to resolve salary and benefit issues. It was a less aggressive method than unions used when it came to working with employers. GE also sent some jobs abroad. In addition, Schenectady's mayor was pushing for more real estate taxes from GE. By 1986 the company's work force was depleted to about 14,000, and the bleeding was not slowing down. Bye-bye, more U.S. jobs. In a city the size of Schenectady with only one main industry, it was not too difficult to realize that "as General Electric goes, so goes the city."

Schenectady was in serious trouble, and it was about to get much worse. In the mid- 1990s, the new tough-on-crime mayor of New York City, Rudy Giuliani, started to push the drug dealers out of the city. Needing a new base from which to operate, the drug dealers looked around and found easy pickings in falling-apart-at-the-seams Schenectady. Urban legend claims that the welfare offices in New York City had signs encouraging welfare recipients to move to upstate New York, where their money would go further because of the cheaper cost of living. The migration was on. Bye-bye, Schenectady.

By 2009 Schenectady's population had dropped to 66,000 with only 3,000 employed at GE, and ALCO long since closed and gone. Schenectady, no longer the city that "lights and hauls" the world. Many of the two-family homes built in the 1920s for GE workers were abandoned, and many more were sagging from years of neglect. The tax base had collapsed due to so many of its citizens being on welfare; and the city services were understaffed, partially because not enough funds were available to pay for everything. Central Park was littered with so much trash that concerned citizens were now volunteering to spend an hour or two, whenever they could, to help clean up what had once been the crown jewel of Schenectady parks.

Today Schenectady has the highest crime rate in New York State, and little optimism can be found amongst the residents that things are going to improve. On the contrary, most believe it is going to get increasingly worse. City officials point to the 24.5 million dollar expansion to Proctors Theatre as the start of a renaissance in a downtown neighborhood; but there were too many empty storefronts, as well as the too few families willing to venture downtown, especially after the sunset, to support the effort. All these things did do not bode well for Schenectady's future. However, as Schenectady attempts to restore itself, people like Neil Golub, chairman of Price Chopper, and restauranteur Angelo Mazzone of Mazzone Hospitality continue to invest their time and treasure in Schenectady and are to be commended, as well as many others, too numerous to be mentioned here.

What Ever Happened to Union College?

If Union ceases to exist, maybe America wouldn't either.

Founded in 1795 as a traditional all-male college, Union started to enroll women in 1970. At the start of 2009, Union College had an undergraduate enrollment of 2,157 students. Its freshman class had 520 students, 240 of them women.

The neighborhood surrounding the campus had seen better days. Because of what some have described as a "sketchy" neighborhood, Union College does not provide visitors with the most direct route to the campus but sends them on the "scenic route", which avoids the meaner streets of an aging and sometimes scary Schenectady. Union College has helped in the revitalization of downtown Schenectady by purchasing and restoring some 25 neglected, former stately houses across from the campus. Union also purchased an "on its last leg" Ramada Inn and converted it into new dorms.

The city of Schenectady and Union College have always had kind of a love-hate relationship, which is true of many college towns. Union is a private institute and is very expensive to attend. Some locals view the students as just a bunch of privileged rich kids. In 1910 the college began erecting a tall, magnificent, ornamental iron fence around the entire 120-acre campus. It became a symbol of its aloof posture towards the city. In a Princeton Review survey, Union College placed second in the nation for "strained town-gown relations."

The pristine grounds of Union are extremely well maintained. They include Jackson's Garden, an eight-acre piece of tranquility located on the northern side of the campus. The garden was started in the 1830s by Professor Isaac Jackson. He took care of the garden until his death. For the next 48 years his daughter Julia took up the task. Julia considered the gardens her personal property and often chased students out. Once from her balcony, that overlooked the garden, she fired a shotgun to scare away visitors to the garden that she deemed not worthy to view the gardens.

Union College is Schenectady's oldest hallowed ground; and if it ever ceases to exist, Schenectady might also cease to exist... maybe America, too.

WHAT EVER HAPPENED TO MONT PLEASANT HIGH SCHOOL?

Mont Pleasant High School

The brick and mortar are still there.

Mont Pleasant High School is now a middle school (7th-8th grade) with 561 students attending. The building still looks the same, but what goes on inside would scare the pants off most of the students who attended high school there in the 1950s. Mont Pleasant Middle School has some of the lowest test scores in the state of New York, and at time the this book was written the discipline problems were out of control.

In October of 2003, Mont Pleasant Middle School permanently suspended 18 students after a rush of bad behavior, including an all-girl, off-campus fight club started simply to see who was the "baddest". Some of the girls involved were 16 years old and still in middle school because they had been held back so often. Neighbors of the school say dismissal time is a mad house. It is not just the students that are the problem; parents have been seen fighting other parents as well.

So the brick and mortar still exists, but never again will the words of the alma mater be proudly sung in its halls:

Mont Pleasant to you our voices we raise, Through all future years we'll echo your praise; Your columns, your tower will always remain,

To recall joyous hours, close friendships we gain; We enter to learn rules and ideals,

We go forth to serve mankind's appeals; Proudly stands our Alma Mater!

WHAT EVER HAPPENED TO NOTT TERRACE HIGH SCHOOL?

Nott Terrace High School

Goodbye Terrace

In 1903, Schenectady High School was built at the cost of $82,420 and was planned for 480 students. By 1909 it was bursting at the seams with 756 students. Schenectady's population in 1900 was 38,682; by 1910 it had jumped to 76,628. In 1911 the high school had an enrollment of 1,000 and could not cope with the increasing student population. The problem was solved by constructing a companion building next to the existing school and joining them together by a second-floor enclosed walkway.

Nott Terrace High School was closed midway through the school year in 1958 and its students transferred to a brand new school named Linton High School. This new school was nationally regarded as an outstanding school. It was located at 1445 The Plaza, about 1½ miles from the old Nott Terrace High School.

In August 1962 the south building of Nott Terrace High School lay in partial ruins, and the demolition contractor had filed a suit against the city, claiming that some of the salvageable items to which he was entitled had been removed. The school property had been part of a 22 block urban renewal project and the school was being demolished to allow Eastern Avenue and Liberty Street to be aligned with each other. In 1974, after the realtor who purchased the property had been unable to sell the site to a developer because of the existing building, the north building of the high school was torn down. The site is now home to a Denny's Restaurant.

As Nott Terrace's Alma Mater was sung in the hallways on the last day before transferring to the new high school, many a tear was shed by students and teachers alike.

Every son of noble Union loves her veiled walls so gray, And the robes and prestige mantles her proud halls for aye; But we claim as fair a mother and to her we will be true,

Nott Terrace High school we love no other than the fairest white and blue. Like a silver star of heaven, Alma Mater ever dear,
  Leading onto mystic Knowledge, guiding through each changing year; In thy dusty tones we glory and the wisdom ever knew,
  In their song and ancient story of the fairest white and blue; When the world of duty calls us from the halls we love so well, When friendship ties are broken and our future none could tell;
  Help us, you dear Alma Mater, to live pure, right wrong, speak true, Like the noble Knights of Arthur for the fairest white and blue.

Goodbye Terrace...Always we'll remember you...Your crowded cafeteria...Hikes to the third floor...The casual Friday night dances... Steadfast Terrace guards...Secret fourth floor... Romances on the bridge...Blue and white...Spirited Election Day Dance...Imposing Campaign Posters...Treks to the field...Gems on the lockers... Portable Student Store...Temperamental water fountains...Tons of trophies...Gala TOP...Waving across the alley...Thanks for the lessons learned.

WHAT EVER HAPPENED TO THE RIVALRY?

So what was so special?

What was so special about the Mont Pleasant-Nott Terrace rivalry? It was not even close to being the oldest high school rivalry - that honor being held by two Massachusetts high schools, Wellesley High School vs. Needham High School. Their rivalry started in 1882, and they have played every Thanksgiving Day since then. The Schenectady rivalry didn't have the most fans in attendance either. The highest number in attendance at an Election Day game was 10,000+, nowhere near the fan base that exists for the rivalry between Trinity High School and St. Xavier's High School in Louisville, Kentucky. They play on the first Friday of October at the University of Louisville Papa John's Cardinal Stadium and typically draw over 35,000 fans.

Even though it wasn't the oldest or highest attended, the Mont Pleasant-Nott Terrace rivalry was still very special to Schenectady. First of all, let's clear up something. There were two distinct rivalries, not one. The first one, from 1932 to 1957, was between Mont Pleasant High School and Nott Terrace High School. The record for those 25 years was Mont Pleasant 15, Nott Terrace 8, with one tie, and one game canceled. Sixteen of the first games were played at Union College's Alexander Field, with the exception of one game being played at Mont Pleasant in 1940 because Alexander Field was being refurbished. The next five games were played at McNearney Stadium, and the last game they played was back at Alexander Field in 1957. The highest attendance for the 24 game rivalry was in 1953 with over 10,000 fans watching Terrace win 19-0, breaking Pleasant's seven-game winning streak with what Coach Shulha called the greatest team he had ever coached. Terrace finished that season undefeated, outscoring its opponents 277-6. *This* is the rivalry that the old-timers in Schenectady remember.

Then Linton High School opened in the middle of the school year in 1957 and Nott Terrace closed its doors forever. As far as the Nott Terrace old-timers were concerned, a new rivalry started in 1958 between Mont Pleasant and Linton, and it was not as intense as the rivalry had been during the first 25 years. The 1958 game was played at Alexander Field and Mont Pleasant won 25-0. That was the last game of the rivalry ever played at Alexander Field. The next two games were played at the Mont Pleasant High School football field, and from then on they see-sawed back and forth between the two schools' home fields. All of the games were played on Election Day until 1970. Then the game day was switched to Saturday because of pressure from the New York State Department of Education to reduce the number of half days of school. In 1972 they went back to Election Day until 1983, when the games were held on Veterans Day until 1985, the year of the last rivalry game between the schools. Mont Pleasant and Linton had played for 28 years with a record of Mont Pleasant 18, Linton 9, and one tie in 1966. The combined attendance for the 28 games was 142,300. Their highest-attended game was in 1963 with almost 8,000 in attendance; Mont Pleasant won 27-6 at Linton that year. Their lowest attendance was 2,000 for the final rivalry game, in which Linton won 33-0 on their home field. The guys from Linton High School felt just as strongly as the Nott Terrace guys had about their rivalry with Mont Pleasant; but for the Mont Pleasant people it was just never the same. But, be that as it may, the rivalry was over. The archrivals would never play each other again.

A rivalry of 53 years is really not that long. So what was so special? It was Schenectady's exclusively—nobody else could claim any part of it. Most of the boys from Schenectady knew they weren't going to college; so if they had a lifelong team and a rivalry, this was it. They held on to it well after finishing high school. You just couldn't take it away from them. It was theirs.

In 1985 the powers that be at Mont Pleasant High School—Coach Dick Serapilio, Athletic Director Ted Thomson, and Principal Louis Mauro—knew it was best for Mont Pleasant football to drop out of the Big Ten High School Conference. The enrollment at Mont Pleasant was so low they could no longer field a competitive team to play against the other Big Ten schools with much higher enrollments. The other schools were Albany, Troy, Amsterdam, Linton, LaSalle, Christian Brothers Academy, Bishop Maginn, Bishop Gibbons, and Catholic Central. It was a controversial decision because now Mont Pleasant could no longer play Linton without being accused of "picking and choosing" their opponents. So there was no Mont Pleasant-Linton game in 1986 and 1987. In 1988 the two schools combined their athletic teams, and high school sports no longer existed at Mont Pleasant. Then in 1992 the schools merged into one at Linton and changed the name to Schenectady High School. Ironically, that was the name of Nott Terrace High School before Mont Pleasant High School was opened in 1931. The rivalry was not only dead, but now it was buried.

Mary Ann Foley, nee Franchetti, had what is possibly the only remaining copy in existence of the official program for the scheduled November 2, 1954, Nott Terrace-Mont Pleasant football game. The near-pristine copy had been kept in her high school scrapbook for the past 60 years. The eight-page program has pictures of both squads and listed by name all of the players, coaches, officials, team managers, and cheerleaders. In the centerfold, which is denoted by a full-color advertisement for Coca-Cola, it showed 18 examples of referee signals. It also contains 22 advertisements for local businesses, with Don Eddy's men's shop taking the entire back page. (If you were really "cool", Don Eddy's hip clothes were part of your wardrobe.) There were eight school cheers, four from each team, on pages two and seven, and a write-up on both teams' 1954 record up to that point. In all of the interviews and research for this book, another copy of this program has not been seen or heard of. Mary Ann graciously donated her treasured copy to the Hall of Fame Museum in Schenectady for its presentation and display. It can currently be seen in the Hall of Fame Mont Pleasant-Nott Terrace Tribute display at Schenectady High School.

Schenectady's Cross-town Football Rivalry

1932 MP 25   NT 0   (at Union's
Alexander Field - 11/8)

- A crowd of approximately 6,000 witnessed Fred
Corky" Stanton pass, run and kick MP to victory in the
inaugural crosstown game. Don Thelan (MP) scored the
first TD in series history. MP, coached by Sig Makofski,
scored 19 fourth quarter points.

1933 MP 20   NT 0   (at Alexander
Field - 11/7)

- An estimated crowd of 6,000 watched in inclement
weather as MP remained undefeated & unscored
upon. John Gorecki scored two MP touchdowns. MP
finished the season undefeated & unscored upon.

1934 MP 6   NT 0   (at Alexander
Field - 11/6)

- 7,000 people witnessed Stanley Kruszewski (MP) score
the game's only TD in a driving rainstorm (ankle deep
mud in some areas of the field).

1935 NT 13   MP 6   (at Alexander
Field - 11/5)

- Nearly 10,000 fans saw Fran Francis score NT's first
points in the series. Francis scores both NT touchdowns.

1936 NT   13   MP   6   (at Alexander
Field - 11/3)

- 10,000 fans watched as NT captain Steve Mashuta
threw the winning touchdown pass in the fourth
quarter. NT finished the season unbeaten.

1937 NT   6   MP   0   (at Alexander
Field - 11/2)

- Close to 8,000 fans saw Steve Mashuta complete a
touchdown pass to Steve Sharkey as NT defeated
MP. Nott Terrace finished 6-0-2.

1938 NT   6   MP   0   (at Alexander
Field - 11/8)

- 10,000 people saw NT win its first game of the
season. It was the fourth consecutive win in the series
for the Blue Devils.

1939 MP   19   NT   0   (at Alexander
Field - 11/7)

 - Between 6,000 and 7,000 people watched as MP
dominated the game, holding NT to just two first
downs. MP finished undefeated.

1940 MP   6   NT   2   (at MP - 11/5)

- Close to 7,000 fans saw MP's Doug Creasy score the
winning touchdown with about three minutes remaining.

1941 NT   6   MP   0   (at Alexander
Field - 11/4)

- Both teams entered the game undefeated for the first
time. County scoring leader Leroy Siegel led a fourth
quarter NT drive and scored from the one. NT finished
undefeated & evened the series at five wins
apiece. (Attendance - 6,000)

1942 MP   26   NT   7   (at Alexander
Field - 11/3)

- Bud Cascini scored two first half touchdowns to propel
MP to victory. Mont Pleasant remained undefeated in
front of 6,500 people.

1943 MP   0   NT   0   [tie]   (at
Alexander Field - 11/6)

- 4,000 fans witnessed the first tie in the series.

1944 NT   13   MP   0   (at Alexander
Field - 11/4)

- Between 5,000 & 6,000 saw Stan Siegel and Eddie
Smialek score NT touchdowns. The NT victory evened
the series.

1945 NT   10   MP   7   (at Alexander
Field - 11/6)

- Ed Gejay scored all NT's points in front of an

estimated 7,000 people (TD pass from Ken Johnson, the PAT, and the game winning FG with three minutes remaining).

1946 MP   7   NT   0   (at Alexander Field - 11/5)

- Ed Dempsey scored the only TD and kicked the extra point as MP evened the series in front of 7,000 fans.

1947 MP   7   NT   6   (at Alexander Field - 11/4)

- Jack Jeffers scored on a 20-yard TD run for MP in the 4th quarter to tie the game & sophomore Tony Parisi ran for the extra point to give MP the series lead. (5,500 fans attended the game.)

1948 MP   19   NT   0   (at Alexander Field - 11/2)

- Each team entered the game with just one loss. More than 9,000 fans watched as Tony Parisi scored twice & kicked an extra point to lead MP to victory.

1949 MP   20   NT   6   (at Alexander Field - 11/5)

 - Tony Parisi, George Kozak & Jack Jeffers scored touchdowns for undefeated MP. These same three players shared the county scoring title. (Attendance - 5,000)

1950 MP   28   NT   13   (at Alexander
Field - 11/7)

- Jack Hamilton scored three touchdowns to lead MP to
its fifth consecutive victory in the series. (Attendance -
7,000)

1951 MP   18   NT   6   (at
Schenectady Stadium - 11/6)

- Walt Jablonski scored three first-half touchdowns in
MP's victory. He ran for 238 yards on 23 carries. MP
finished the season with just one loss. Jablonski scored
14 touchdowns in six games and led the Capital District
in scoring. (Attendance - 7,000)

1952 MP   27   NT   7   (at
Schenectady Stadium - 11/4)

- Don Giagiacomo (Como), the county scoring
champion, scored three touchdowns and propelled MP to
its seventh consecutive victory vs. NT. Como had 180
yards in 19 carries. Larry Mulvaney's first MP team tied
for the Class "A" League title. (Attendance - 6,000)

1953 NT   19   MP   0   (at
Schenectady Stadium - 11/3)

- The greatest football team in NT history broke MP's
seven game winning streak in the series. NT was led by
fullback Derry Cooke & All American guard Bob
Czub. NT won the Class "A" League title and finished

undefeated, outscoring its opponents 277-6. (Attendance - estimated over 10,000)

1954   (No game - polio outbreak)

- Each team finished undefeated. MP (5-0) outscored its opponents 171-6. NT (5-0 & undefeated for the second consecutive year) outscored its opponents 193-33. The Election Day game was canceled after Dan Monaco, MP's co-captain & fullback, contracted polio just days before the game. Oliver DeVito, a Nott Terrace halfback, also contracted polio. Each team had one additional game canceled.

1955 MP   21   NT   0   (at Schenectady Stadium - 11/8)

- Jim Poirier threw two first half touchdown passes as MP won its tenth consecutive game (dating back to '54). MP won the Class "A" League championship & finished undefeated for the second consecutive year. (Estimated. attendance - 8,000)

1956 MP   51   NT   12   (at Schenectady Stadium- 11/6)

- League champion MP gained over 500 yards as it won the most lop-sided game in series history. Eddie Ferraro (MP) had TD runs of 54 & 58 yards. All American Gary Trout, Robb Ogilvie & Carm Pantalone also starred for MP. Carl McNeal (NT) had a 98 yard kickoff return. (Attendance - 5,300)

1957 NT   13   MP   7   (at
Alexander Field - 11/5)

- NT upset favored MP. Jim Gaetano's QB sneak put
NT ahead for good. Carl McNeal, Jack Hughes, Carm
Ronca & Dick Brainard also starred for NT. It's the last
rivalry game involving NT. (Attendance - 5,000)

1958 MP   25   L   0   (at
Alexander Field - 11/4)

- In the first game played by Linton in the series, Tom
Mahar (MP) scored on two 34-yard TD runs as MP won
the Class "A" League title (undefeated and unscored
upon in league play). (Attendance - 7,000)

1959 MP   33   L   0   (at MP -
11/3)

- 5,500 fans watched as Al Bojarski, Jack Edwards, Ron
Penta, Joe DeMeo & Pat Maney scored touchdowns for
MP. MP remained unbeaten & won the league title
when it broke open a close game with 27 second half
points. (MP lost its final game at White
Plains.)

1960 L   18   MP   0   (at MP -
11/8)

- Dick Wilgocki & Dick Stipano (67 yard TD run) led
the Linton ground attack. Stipano also scored on a 27-
yard fumble recovery and Paul Bricoccoli threw a 15-

yard TD pass to Nick Capra. Linton finished 7-
1. (Attendance - est. 6,000)

1961 L   13   MP   0   (at Linton -
11/7)

- Linton All-American Ron Oyer ran for a 12-yard TD &
threw a TD pass to Dan DeMeo. Linton won the Class
"A" League championship and finished 7-1. No Section
II team scored on Linton. (Attendance - 6,000)

1962 MP   14   L   13   (at MP -
11/6)

- An 8-yard TD pass from Frank Pidgeon to Joe
Massaroni with 27 seconds remaining enabled MP to
upset undefeated Linton (with All- American Pat Riley
& Thom McAn Award winner Mike Meola) in perhaps
the most exciting game in the series. MP & Linton tied
for the Class "A" League championship. (Attendance -
5,000)

1963 MP   27   L   6   (at Linton -
11/5)

- Powerful fullback Ralph Moore scored two
touchdowns as MP ended Linton's 1963 five game
winning streak. Speedy All-American halfback Paul
Della Villa, the county scoring champion, also starred
for MP. The MP defense forced six LHS fumbles &
blocked a punt for a TD. MP won the Class "A" League
title. (Attendance - almost 8,000)

1964 MP   19   L   7   (at MP - 11/3)

- Emery Moore rushed for 158 yards on 11 carries, including a 98 yard TD run in the closing minutes to secure MP's victory. (Attendance - 6,000)

1965 MP   27   L   14   (at Linton 11/2)

- Red Raider Emery Moore scored on TD runs of 63, 61 & 35 yards as MP won the rivalry game for the fourth consecutive year. (Attendance 4,500)

1966 L   6   MP 6   (at MP - 11/8)

- The game ended in a tie for the second time in series history. John Campbell (L) & Ron Page (MP) each scored a touchdown. Linton & MP shared the Class "A" League title. Linton finished undefeated (6-0-1). (Attendance - 6,000)

1967 MP   27   L   13   (at Linton - 11/7)

- Both teams entered the game undefeated in the league. MP, ahead 14-13, scored two 4th quarter touchdowns to secure the victory. Dennis Pelkey (MP) scored two touchdowns. Ron Page (126 yds. on 25 carries) & Harold Oppelt also scored MP touchdowns. MP finished 8-0, won the Class "A" League and was voted #1 in NYS.

Other notable Red Raiders included All-American Gale Knull, co-capt. Al Aldi & future nationally acclaimed movie producer, John Sayles. (Attendance - over 7,000)

1968 MP   14   L   13   (at MP - 11/5)

- A crowd of 6,500 watched as QB Ken Wachowicz scored a touchdown in the 3rd period & Jerry Carlos added the extra point to give MP a 14-13 lead and the victory. All-American Ron Page also scored a TD for MP. The Red Raiders won the Class "A" League (undefeated in league play).

1969 L   6   MP   0   (at Linton - 11/4)

- Linton surprised MP behind the outstanding play of All-American Ken Grey. Grey scored the only touchdown & was selected as the game's outstanding defensive player (9 tackles & 9 assists). MP tied for the Class "A" League championship. (Attendance - est. 6,500)

1970 MP   12   L   0   (at MP - Sat. 11/7)

- Marc DellaVilla caught two touchdown passes from Bob DeGasperis to lead MP to victory. (Attendance - 5,000)

1971 L   26   MP   7   (at Linton -

Sat. 11/6)

- Brian Rossler, Rodney Palmer, Ernie LaBier & John Sykes (the future president of VH1) scored Linton's touchdowns. Bernie Torres led an outstanding effort by the Blue Devils' defense. The Saturday game drew one of the series' smallest crowds - perhaps 4,500.

1972 MP   23   L   0   (at MP - 11/7)

- The rivalry game was once again played on Election Day. Approximately 6,500 fans watched as Mark DiDonato threw TD passes to Orin Griffin & John DeMeo. DeMeo also ran for a TD. The Red Raiders won the Class "A" League championship.

1973 L   9   MP   0   (at Linton - 11/6)

- Linton upset MP in front of 6,000 people. Jim Ring excelled for the Blue Devils. Frank Washington scored the game's only TD in the 4th quarter.

1974 MP   12   L   8   (at MP - 11/5)

- With the Red Raiders trailing 8-6, MP's Mike Palmer threw a 31 yard TD pass to Dick Holoday with 1:26 remaining in the game. Palmer also scored a TD for MP. Percy Johnson had a TD & a two point conversion for the Blue Devils. (Attendance - 5,000)

1975 L   3   MP   0   (at Linton)

- Alan Darling kicked a 30-yd. FG in the 4th quarter as Linton defeated MP & won a share of the Class "A" League title. (Attendance - 6,500)

1976 MP   14   L   8   (at MP - 11/2)

- Jim Donahue scored a TD and threw a TD pass to Terrance Williams as MP won the last rivalry game played on Election Day. It was also Larry Mulvaney's last crosstown rivalry game. Tony Affinito scored Linton's TD. Williams & Affinito each gained nearly 150 yards on the ground. (Attendance - over 4,000)

1977 MP   12   L   8   (at Linton - 11/11)

- Trailing 8-7 in the fourth quarter, Rick Boni kicked a 20-yard FG to give MP the lead. MP won for the first time at Linton since 1967.   (Attendance - 3,500)

1978 MP   28   L   14   (at MP - 11/10)

- Ricky Boyd (171 yards in 19 carries) ran for three third quarter touchdowns as MP pulled away from Linton. Tim Kennedy starred on defense for Red Raiders. (Attendance - est. 3,500)

1979 MP   20   L   0   (at Linton -

11/12)

- John Sawchuk scored two first half touchdowns to lead the Red Raiders to victory in front of a crowd of 2,500.

1980 MP   14   L   9   (at MP -
11/11)

- Vinnie Savini threw two second quarter TD passes to Mike Gartley as MP won its fifth consecutive game in the series. (Attendance - 3,000)

1981 L   33   MP   14   (at Linton -
11/14)

- Sean Messitt (L) scored two touchdowns & rushed for 148 yards on 20 carries. John Palmiotto (fumble recovery) & Jeff Woodard (interception return) also scored Linton touchdowns. Joe Capra (MP) blocked two punts, each resulting in a TD. (Attendance - est. 2,300)

1982 MP   10   L   7   (at MP -
11/11)

- In the 50th game in the football rivalry, John Greco broke a 7-7 tie when he kicked a 25-yard FG in the fourth quarter. Todd Williams (127 yards on 30 carries) scored MP's touchdown. Kyle Siegel (L) rushed for 112 yards in the first half, including a 67 yard TD run. (Attendance - 3,500)

1983 MP   37   L   7   (at Linton -

11/11)

- Running backs Joe Marra & Todd Williams combined for 187 yards & three touchdowns as MP defeated Linton in a steady rain. (Attendance - nearly 3,000)

1984 L   14   MP   0   (at MP - 11/12)

- Brian Borowski & Ray Schiavo scored fourth quarter touchdowns as Linton defeated the Red Raiders for the first time at MP since 1960. Schiavo was a two-way standout for Linton. (Attendance - 2,500)

1985 L   33   MP   0   (at Linton - 11/11)

- Flanker Vince Pedone caught two TD passes from Jim Poirier as Linton   won the final game in the series. It was the most lopsided win by the Blue Devils in the 53 games played by the city rivals. MP was held to 75 yards in total offense on a cold, rainy day. Tony Mammola (L) scored the final point in the series, a PAT following a Chris Brown TD.   (Attendance - 2,000)

OVERALL: **Mont Pleasant** - 33 victories

Nott Terrace / Linton - 18 victories (nine by each school)

(Two ties)

COACHING RECORDS:

Mont Pleasant

Sig Makofski	6-5
Nick Reig	1-2-1
George Van Heusen	5-0
Larry Mulvaney	14-7-1
Tony Parisi	1-1
Dick Serapilio	6-3

Nott Terrace / Linton

Erwin Clark	5-6-1
Whitey Boehm	2-1
Pete Shulha	2-8
Walt Przybylo	0-1
Bill Eaton	0-1
Dick Lalla	2-2
Spencer Sullivan	0-2

Gerry Baker   5-7-1

Hugo Bach   0-1

Ted Thomson   2-4

Information found in the Daily Gazette, the Union Star, the Knickerbocker News & the Linton Hi-Lights. Compiled by Schenectady City School District Athletic Hall of Fame and Reunion Dinner.

What Ever Happened to Polio?

Ninety-nine percent decrease

In April of 1955 the Salk vaccine was proclaimed to be the preventative polio miracle drug that the public had anxiously awaited since the early 1900s. Doctors Jonas Salk and Albert Sabin worked separately using donations to the March of Dimes from millions of people, totaling over $25,000,000 (which would be well over 200 million in today's dollars), for their vaccine research and development. These two men were the principal leaders of the scientific teams whose work led to the essential eradication of this disease.

Fifty years later, the Smithsonian National Museum of American History in Washington D.C. opened its year-long exhibition entitled, "What Ever Happened to Polio?" Dr. Salk received great public recognition for his deactivated or killed virus vaccine, but by 1962, Dr. Sabin's live virus vaccine became the choice for use in the United States. The Salk vaccine was injected while the Sabin vaccine was given orally, making it cheaper to produce and greatly reducing the fear factor for the recipients, who were mostly younger children. The annual number of polio cases fell from 35,000 in 1953 to 5,600 in 1957. By 1961, only 161 cases were reported in the United States; however, in 2000, after several live virus vaccinations resulted in cases of polio, Sabin's vaccine was superseded by Salk's. The Smithsonian exhibit emphasizes that the worldwide prevention of polio would not have been successfully accomplished without both the research and discoveries of both Doctors Salk and Sabin.

The last case of polio caused by a "wild" or naturally occurring virus was reported in the U.S. in 1979. In 1988, when the Global Polio Eradication Initiative began, more than 1,000 children worldwide were still being paralyzed by polio on a daily basis. Since then, more than 2.5 billion children have been immunized against polio, backed by an investment of more than nine billion dollars, or about $3.60 per immunization. There are now only three countries—Afghanistan, Pakistan, and Nigeria—that have never succeeded in stopping polio transmission, and worldwide occurrences of polio cases have decreased by 99 percent.

In the 1990s, physicians identified Post-Polio Syndrome (PPS) in people who had the disease. Post-Polio Syndrome is a condition that affects polio survivors years after having recovered from the initial acute attack of the virus. In the syndrome, polio survivors most often start to experience gradual new weakening in muscles that had been previously affected by the polio infection. Like polio itself, there is no cure for PPS, but some studies suggest that non-fatiguing exercises may improve muscle strength and reduce tiredness for those suffering from this condition.

In the United States, most people are given the polio vaccines when they are children. A deactivated polio virus (Salk's vaccine) is injected into the leg or arm depending on the patient's age. Polio vaccines can be administered simultaneously with other vaccines. Children usually receive four doses of Inactivated Polio Vaccine at the ages of 2 months, 4 months, and 6-18 months, with a booster dose at 4-6 years.

NAME INDEX

(First Mention)

ACKNOWLEDGEMENTS

———◆———

I WANT TO THANK THREE members of my family who together tran-scribed and edited my book: my granddaughter, Maddy Lee, who somehow was able to read my handwriting and then type my man-uscript; my oldest daughter, Sheila Meneses, who did the first edit and helped me polish my writing; and my wife, Colleen, who did the painstaking final edit. Mike Petrolle greatly assisted me with his extraordinary memory of the games and the times. I also want to thank Bob Pezzano, the Chairman of Schenectady City Athletic Hall of Fame, who helped me find so many people I needed to interview that I had almost given up on locating; and Tony Cristello, Schenectady's hometown artist par excellence, for allowing me to use his magnificent painting entitled, "An Unfilled Dream", as the cover for my book. From the first time I saw the painting, it was my only choice for the cover. Thank you all.

SPECIAL ACKNOWLEDGEMENT

———◆———

WITHOUT THE SCHENECTADY UNION STAR and the Schenectady Gazette Sports Departments, reporting the games would have been impossible. To describe the play by play action of the football games played-by-Mont Pleasant and Nott Terrace in their 1954 seasons, I used a combination of both newspapers' articles, coaches, players and fans remembrances to reconstruct the games.

ABOUT THE AUTHOR

AS A HIGH SCHOOL FRESHMAN, Dennis R. Bender was an eyewitness to many of the events recounted in *Like It Was Yesterday*. He and his wife, Colleen, have been married for 35 years and now live in Saint Petersburg, Florida.

Dennis and Colleen Bender

Made in the USA
Middletown, DE
06 January 2021